T0380670

DYNAMIC STUDIES

IN THE LETTERS OF
JOHN AND JUDE

BRINGING GOD'S WORD TO LIFE

FRED A. SCHEEREN

WESTBOW
PRESS®
A DIVISION OF THOMAS NELSON
& ZONDERVAN

WestBow Press books may be ordered through booksellers or by contacting:

WestBow Press
A Division of Thomas Nelson & Zondervan
1663 Liberty Drive
Bloomington, IN 47403
www.westbowpress.com
844-714-3454

ISBN: 979-8-3850-2578-7 (sc)
ISBN: 979-8-3850-2579-4 (e)

Library of Congress Control Number: 2024910586

Print information available on the last page.

WestBow Press rev. date: 07/08/2024

DEDICATION

I DEDICATE THIS book to my lovely wife, Sally, who is a Jewish believer and Ivy League educated attorney. She has stood by me over the years and raised our sons in our God-loving home. The comfort of sharing our friendship and our love for Christ has encouraged me greatly in creating this series of dynamic studies of various books of the Bible. Sally's participation in our small group studies has added a much deeper dimension of richness to the discussions. Thank you for sharing your heritage, training, and knowledge.

CONTENTS

ACKNOWLEDGMENTS

MY FRIEND, BOB Mason, who at the time I began the Dynamic Bible Studies series, was in his second career as the pastor of small groups at the Bible Chapel in the South Hills of Pittsburgh, suggested the overall structure of each study. Realizing our group was doing more in-depth work than most, he asked that I include several important segments in each lesson—most specifically, the warm-up and life application phases.

Bob suggested a great resource called the *New Testament Lesson Planner* from InterVarsity Press. I have augmented this with commentaries by Dr. Charles Missler from Koinonia House, the *Wiersbe Bible Commentary*, *The MacArthur Bible Handbook* by Dr. John MacArthur, the *Bible Commentaries* of J. Vernon McGee, and the whole of Scripture itself. To make the utilization of the whole of Scripture more efficient, I have also leaned heavily on the Libronix Digital Library, perhaps the most advanced Bible software available, and other resources to help us understand how the New Testament and the Tanakh (Old Testament) fit together as one cohesive document.

I have also enjoyed the encouragement of my friend, Ron Jones, as I have continued to prepare these studies. Ron is a former high school principal and administrator. He is also a committed believer and daily student of God's Word. His background in education coupled with his love of God and His Word has made him a powerful force for good.

I would like to express thanks to my late friend, Gordon Haresign, for his continued support and encouragement in my efforts to produce the Dynamic Bible Studies series. Gordon's journey began with his birth in the Belgian Congo. In the following years he was a senior executive with an international accounting firm, served in the military, labored as a Bible college professor, was instrumental in the leadership of a worldwide Bible correspondence school, and most recently served as the Chairman of the Board of Directors of Scripture Union, an international Bible-based ministry. Gordon's work as a teacher, speaker, and missionary took him to over 50 countries on five continents. His three most recent books, *Authentic Christianity*, *Pray for the Fire to Fall* and his last work on Paul's letters to the Thessalonians which may someday be in print, should be required reading for all believers. Speaking of the Dynamic Bible Studies series he wrote, "These are among the finest, if not the finest, inductive Bible studies available today. I strongly endorse them."

I would also like to express my appreciation to my contributing editor, Cynthia Nicastro. Cindy is an intelligent, ardent and devoted student of the Scriptures and a meticulous grammarian.

May God bless you, inspire you, teach you, and change your life for the better as you work through these lessons.

PREFACE

Welcome to what I hope you find to be a most enjoyable and enlightening study. The first subjects are the letters of John. These are quite instructive and should have great impact on the lives of believers as they apply God's Word to their lives.

The second subject of this study is the letter of Jude. This quite appropriately follows the letters of John. It details experiences believers in today's world will have as they apply the lessons found in John's letters and the rest of the God's Word. As such, it is a great aid in preparing believers to survive and thrive in the times that are ahead.

As we consider how this book of the Bible fits into the whole of the New Testament and the Tanakh (the name used by Jews for the Old Testament, used here to emphasize the Jewishness of the Scriptures), we need to realize a number of things. We should stand in awe of this collection of 66 books, written over thousands of years by at least 40 different authors. Every detail of the text is there by design. It explains history before it happens, and comes to us from outside the dimension of time. It is, in short, the most amazing, most authenticated, and most accurate book available in the world.

If this claim is not strong enough, add to it the indisputable fact that the words contained therein have changed more lives than any others now in existence.

While the Judeo-Christian Scriptures are demonstrably perfect, my prepared studies are not. There is no way I or anyone else could possibly incorporate the depth of the text into individual sessions. I simply desire to provide a vehicle for others to use in their investigation of the Scriptures as they incorporate these timeless truths into their lives.

Speaking of small groups, Dr. Chuck Missler, a former Fortune 500 CEO, said, "I experienced more growth in my personal life as a believer by participating in small group Bible studies than anything else." I believe you may find this to be true in your experience and encourage you to be an active participant in such a mutually supportive, biblically-based group.

GROUND RULES

I DESIGNED THE first portion of each study to encourage readers to think about their personal situation. I designed the second portion to help people understand what the text says and how it relates to the whole of Scripture. And finally, each lesson ends with a discussion designed to help people apply that lesson.

You will notice that, in most instances, I have included the citation, but not the actual text of the Scripture we are considering. I did this on purpose. I believe we all learn more effectively if we have to dig out the text itself. As a byproduct of that exercise, we become more familiar with this marvelous book.

Scripture references are preceded or followed by a question or series of questions. Again, this is on purpose. I have also found that people seem to learn most effectively when employing the Socratic Method. That is, instead of telling someone what the text says and how it relates to other texts and life, they will remember it better if they answer questions about it and ferret out the information for themselves.

In a few instances, I have inserted additional commentary or partial answers to some of the questions to help the group get the most out of the study.

It is my intention and suggestion that the various scripture references be read out loud as part of each session. Shorter passages might be read by one participant, while anything over two or three verses might serve everyone better if one member reads one verse and another reads the next until the passage is completed. This keeps everyone involved. After reading these passages, I intend that how they relate to the primary Scripture at hand be seriously considered. At times, this relationship seems to be available and obvious on the surface. In many other instances, the interconnectedness of the whole of Scripture and its principles are most effectively understood through deeper thought, discussion, and prayer.

In commenting on and discussing the various passages, questions, concepts, and principles in this material, it is not required that any particular person give his or her input. The reader of any passage may, but is not pressured to, give his or her thoughts to the group. This is a group participation exercise for the mutual benefit of all involved and many people in the group giving their insight into a certain verse or question will often enhance the learning experience.

I also have two practical suggestions if you work through this book in a small group setting. Every time you meet, I suggest you review the calendar and agree upon the next scheduled meeting as well as who will bring refreshments. This will help the group to run a lot more smoothly while enhancing everyone's enjoyment, experience, and expectations.

Introduction to the
Letters of John

After speaking with my excellent contributing editor, Cynthia Nicastro, it is obvious that I should answer her first question before continuing. She is a great and intelligent member of our team so I am sure this same query will be repeated by those utilizing and hopefully enjoying this book. Her question is; "Why would you begin a study of this nature with 3 John followed by 2 John and then 1 John. Doesn't it make more sense to do it in the order in which we find these letters in the Bible itself?"

This is certainly a very good question. And, I have to admit that I struggled with the issue of how to present this material myself when preparing these studies. I suppose the best answer is that when reviewing the material, the third and second letters provide a perfect prelude to the first letter. They illustrate the difficulties and triumphs experienced by these first century believers in brief. As such, they lay the groundwork for 1 John which takes on the challenge of responding to difficulties and false teachers in greater and very effective detail.

I take comfort that the man many consider to be the greatest Biblical scholar of all time, Dr. Charles Missler, who preferred to be called Chuck, ended up taking this same approach. I fully realize that in calling Chuck the greatest we are making a bold statement as there are so many wonderful people being used and who have been used by God in this arena. Certainly, the apostle Paul, likely the most intelligent, highly educated and well-read man of his time would be a primary contender. Chuck had the advantage of having the fullness of the written Scriptures at hand which may have given him a leg up. Either way, we are thankful for each of these fine men as well as all legitimate and honest students of God's Word.

This short series deals with a number of what are known as the New Testament Epistles. In particular we will begin with the three Epistles of John. John, a disciple of Jesus Christ, was one of the original twelve apostles and, on a personal level, is thought to be the person Jesus knew best. He is the author of no fewer than five books of the New Testament. This amounts to 8.3% of the New and Old Testaments combined and 20% of the books of the New Testament. The books he authored include, *The Gospel of John, The First Letter of John, the Second Letter of John, the Third Letter of John, and the Revelation of Jesus Christ.*

The *Third Letter of John* and the *Second Letter of John* are personal missives with broader implications as part of God's Word. The *First Letter of John* has often been called the sanctum sanctorum of the New Testament. It is, in many ways, more important to the life of the believer than all the other letters of the New Testament. This is quite a statement knowing how vital the remaining letters are to life and health.

Following the structure of Chuck Missler's review of the three short letters of John, we will first discuss and analyze letters three and two, culminating with a study of the first letter, in this order. Dr. Missler felt, and I concur, that this is a most effective way in which to deal with this portion of the Word of God.

When all is said and done, we should realize that:

1. Life is real. It is not a playground or a simple preparation for the future. It is now, it is important, and everything within it has meaning.

2. Life is a battleground. Indeed, a believer has real life now as well as eternal life. Having come to that state, a believer has a more meaningful and impactful life now, regardless of the opposition faced as they essentially bring God's Word and message to the world in which the believer lives.

3. If someone is wrong about Jesus Christ, they are wrong about God.

4. If a person is wrong about God, like it or not, they are wrong on one level or another, about everything else.

As Jesus Christ Himself said in John 14:6 *"I am the way, the truth and the life. Noone comes to the father except through Me."* GNT

And now, as we build the stage for the message of the *First Letter of John*, we will begin with the *Third Letter of John*.

It is a matter of great import and interest that the Church, as comprised of those who have trusted Jesus Christ, has been under attack since its' inception. These attacks have most often emanated from without. However, in some instances, they have occurred from within. These attacks, whether from within or without, have been anticipated by the Holy Spirit. The attacks themselves represent every conceivable and some almost inconceivable forms of diversion, division, misdirection, and supposed scholarship.

Fortunately for us, the Holy Spirit has not only anticipated these attacks, but has made provision for believers to successfully overcome them. This power is available not just through the power of the Holy Spirit Himself, but through God's Word, which He inspired. As we approach the epistles of John we see this brought down to a personal level as we learn from the many situations with which God deals in the text.

Speaking of John, we should remember that he:

1.   Was the brother of James.

     See: .

     - Matthew 4:21.

     - Matthew 10:2.

     - Mark 1:19.

     - Mark 3:17.

     - Mark 10:35.

2.   Was most likely the younger of the sons of Zebedee and Salome.

     See:

     - Matthew 4:21.

     - Matthew 27:56.

     - Mark 15:40.

3.   Was born at Bethsaida.

4.   Was a scion of a wealthy family.

     See:

     - Mark 1:20.

     - Luke 5:3.

     - John 19:27.

5. Surprisingly worked as a fisherman.

6. Seems to have been influenced by the teaching of John the Baptist.

7. Heard about Jesus through the ministry of John the Baptist.

8. Became a follower and disciple of Jesus through John the Baptist.

   See:

   - John 1:36-37.

9. Returned to fishing for an uncertain period of time after making a decision to follow Jesus.

10. Along with his brother made a permanent decision to attach himself to the person and program of Jesus.

    See:

    - Matthew 4:21.

    - Luke 5:1-11.

11. Became, along with his brother, known as Boanerges, translated to Sons of Thunder, because of their zeal and intensity of character and purpose.

    See:

    - Mark 3:17.

    - Matthew 20:20-24.

    - Mark 10:35-41.

    - Luke 9:49, 54.

12. Became part of Jesus' innermost circle as evidenced in Scripture.

    See:

- Mark 5:37.

- Mathew 17:1.

- Matthew 26:37.

- Mark 13:3.

13. Was referred to as the disciple Jesus loved.

    See:

    - John 19:26.

    - John 20:2.

    - John 21:7.

    - John 21:20.

14. Was the person to whose care Jesus consigned his mother.

    See:

    - John 19:26-27

15. Followed Jesus even when others abandoned Him.

    See:

    - John 18:15, 16, 19, 28.

16. Was one of the first disciples to whom Mary gave the news of Jesus' resurrection.

    See:

    - John 20:2.

17. Returned to fishing in the lake of Galilee after Jesus' resurrection, at which place Jesus revealed himself to John and Peter.

    See:

    - John 21:1, 7.

18. Worked closely with Peter in the development of the group of early believers after the resurrection.

    See:

    - Acts 3:1.

    - Acts 4:13.

19. Penned, through the power of the Holy Spirit, the Gospel most oriented toward helping someone understand and then become equipped to follow Jesus Christ.

20. Ultimately penned the last book of the Bible; *Revelation*.

In the Third Letter of John, we first notice that it is addressed to Gaius. This was not an uncommon name at the time. Therefore, today we are not certain if it was addressed to the Gaius:

- In Macedonia (Acts 19:29).

- In Corinth (Romans 16:23).

- In Derbe (Acts 20:4).

This is the shortest letter which we know of John writing. It appears to be written in order to introduce Gauis to a group of believers with whom he was unfamiliar. These people were traveling to the locale in which Gauis found himself for the purpose of sharing the Gospel. As such, the key concepts in the short missive are those relating to bearing witness. We see this in:

3 John:3.

3 John:6.

3 John:12.

We should see from this that every believer is either by definition helping or hindering God's truth. As a corollary to this, it appears that every believer has a choice as to whether they will be part of God's program, plan and solution or part of the problem. God, of course, not only desires positive action and words, but provides the resources for every believer to be part of the solution.

It is my hope that everyone using this material or who otherwise reads the Scriptures in consideration will be blessed by the effort and more thoroughly equipped for life both now and in the future as we see expressed in John 10:10. The NLT says it this way: "The thief's purpose is to steal and kill and destroy. My purpose is to give them a rich and satisfying life."

WEEK 1

GAIUS IS ENCOURAGED
3 JOHN 1-14

Open in Prayer

Group Warm-Up Questions

What gives you the greatest joy in life?

If you are part of a large group of believers, what sort of people within the fellowship are the most highly thought of?

What famous people are currently the objects of malicious gossip in the tabloids?

Read: 3 John:1-14

Reread: 3 John:1

To whom is this letter addressed and from whom is it sent?

What do you think it means to love someone in the truth?

Reread: 3 John:2

For what did John pray and hope? Please make a list.

    1.

    2.

    3.

When it comes down to basic necessities, what more does a person need?

Reread: 3 John:3-4

What two things gave John great joy?

    1.

    2.

Why do you think this gave him such great joy?

How do you feel when someone you have trained or poured your knowledge into responds by putting into practice the truths you have tried to impart?

Please think of and discuss an example.

If other believers were to give a report about you, what do you think they would say?

How might they describe your faithfulness?

What area of life provides the most challenge to you in being faithful?

What about being a believer gives you joy?

Please read Galatians 5:22-23 as you think about your answer.

Reread: 3 John:5

In what specific way was Gaius demonstrating his faithfulness?

Reread: 3 John:6

What did the traveling teachers report back to the believers with whom John was working?

What request did John make of Gaius?

Reread: 3 John:7

What were these traveling teachers doing?

How did these people receive their support?

Why do you think they did not accept any help from nonbelievers?

Do you think they were right in only accepting financial help from believers?

Why or why not?

Note: Many years ago, after I graduated from college, I worked for the Coalition for Christian Outreach. During this period of time, I was also on the staff of two churches, taught college courses, led Bible studies, managed a tutoring system, served as a Resident Director for student housing, served as liaison between a college and their maintenance staff, was instrumental in recalcitrant student discipline, and served as head wrestling coach. It was a surprise to me when a number of coaches, athletes and even an athletic director from various sports and institutions, college professors, as well as nonbelieving business people and even drug dealers, all who knew what I was doing, contributed toward my support. I accepted it and continued in my work.

Do you think I was wrong or right in accepting their support?

How so?

Do you think Christian churches, teachers, and institutions who accept donations from people who may not be completely committed, but appreciate the results of their work, are wrong to accept donations from these people?

They almost all do.

Reread: 3 John:8

What did John say they should do for the traveling teachers who would not accept donations from unbelievers?

Again, do you believe these teachers were short-sighted in not accepting donations that God provided them even through unbelievers? Why?

Note: Whatever your answer, this brings up an interesting point. Different people who are sincere in their faith will respond differently to the question above. The methodology of their raising support and our feelings about it, no matter how well founded, is not a significant point of faith. We must not let insignificant differences become significant in such a way that they interfere with following Jesus, the Jewish Messiah.

Can you think of examples when different people or groups with the same goals did not work together because of disagreement on some insignificant issues did not work together to the detriment of all? Please explain?

Can you think of examples when different people or groups with the same goals worked together toward a common goal? Please explain.

In times of war, what do the citizens of victorious countries with differing opinions on nonessential topics tend to do to insure not only their survival but victory?

Please read the following verses as you contemplate these questions, especially in light of the situation in which believers find themselves in the world.

Philippians 2:2-4

1 Peter 3:8

1 Peter 3:8-17

Romans 15:5-6

James 4:7

1 John 4:4

2 Corinthians 10:3-5

1 Peter 5:8-9

Ephesians 6:10-17

1 Corinthians 10:13

John 8:32

1 Timothy 6:12

Isaiah 40:31

Deuteronomy 3:22

Romans 8:31

Joshua 1:9

Psalm 44:5

John 16:33

Psalm 91:1-4

John 10:10

2 Thessalonians 3:3

Romans 8:37-39

2 Chronicles 20:15

How should we show hospitality to other believers?

Reread: 3 John:9

What did Diotrephes love?

As a result of his wanting to operate independently and under his own authority, what did Diotrephes do?

It was no secret that John was not only knowledgeable, but also one of Jesus' primary apostles. Why, then, might Diotrephes have acted as he did?

In what areas of life do you strive to be first?

Do you feel your efforts are like Diotrephes or are they different?

Please explain?

Reread: 3 John:9-10

What else was Diotrephes doing?

What did John say he would do when he arrived at the fellowship of which both Diotrephes and Gaius were part of?

Why, in today's world, are people often slow or reticent to follow the example of John and the admonition of Scripture to put the divisive or evil person out of their group?

Read the following references to see a short version of what God's Word says about this.

Psalm 26:4-5

1 John 4:1

2 Corinthians 6:14

Matthew 12:35

1 Corinthians 5:11

Proverbs 24:20

1 Corinthians 5:9-13

What happens when a divisive person remains in a group?

Read the following verses as you contemplate your answer.

Proverbs 22:24-25

1 Corinthians 15:33

Proverbs 13:20

Proverbs 14:7

Proverbs 25:26

What happens when sincere believers associate with one another?

Please read the following verses as you think about your answer.

Psalm 1:1-4

Proverbs 3:5-6

Psalm 119:115

Proverbs 27:17

Reread: 3 John:11

What did John tell Gaius to do that was in concert with all the Scriptures we reviewed just now?

In what areas of your life do you need to do better at imitating good rather than evil?

Note: This is an opportune time to review *How to Avoid Error* in the Appendices in this book. Please take a look.

What can a person do to improve their record of faithfulness?

Reread: 3 John:12

What was so commendable about Demetrius?

Reread: 3 John:13-14

Why was the third letter of John so short?

What did John so very much want to do?

Application Questions

In what area of life can you be more faithful this week?

To whom can you show hospitality this week?

In what way will you emulate good behavior instead of evil this very day?

Close in Prayer

TO THE CHOSEN LADY
2 JOHN 1-13

Open in Prayer

Group Warm-Up Questions

Who is someone you have written to most recently?

Why is it often easier to start a new activity than to stick with it?

Read: 2 John:1-13

Reread: 2 John:1

Who wrote this letter?

To whom was this letter written?

Introductory Note: It is thought by most scholars that this letter is figuratively written to the group corporately (the chosen lady) and the followers of Jesus Christ individually (her children) in Ephesus.

Students of ancient history will realize that Ephesus was known as the greatest metropolis in Asia. It had a huge open-air theater that accommodated up to 50,000 people. Indeed, this was as large or larger than many modern sports arenas. By way of comparison, Three Rivers Stadium, which was home to the Pittsburgh Pirates and Steelers from 1970 to 2000, seated 47,971 fans for baseball games, and 59,000 for football games.

This city was where the Gospel was first preached after Pentecost as we see in Acts 2:9 and Acts 6:9.

A number of various groups opposing the truth in Ephesus at the time were generally known as Gnostics. As such they taught that the spiritual world was divine and good while the physical world was evil. A necessary corollary was then that Jesus could not have come in physical form or that he was not divine. (Both claims, of course, run counter to the truth.)

John's second letter certainly encompasses how to deal with these people who are most directly referenced in the text.

As already mentioned, the letter is viewed as being sent to groups, rather than to an individual. This is consistent with the Greek used in the original text. We should also note that in reality, while people most often become believers at least partially as a result of interchange with other believers, they are not really children of the church. They are children of God. (See John 1:12-13.)

We would be remiss, however, if we did not report that certain people wish to interpret the letter as having been written to Mary, the mother of Jesus. This is consistent with ancient Babylonian mythology which has infiltrated the Roman Catholic Church. Most of this has been contrived by various popes with little Biblical or historical basis.

Nevertheless, we did say there was some Biblical basis for thinking this letter was written to Mary, the human mother of Jesus. We see:

1.   Mary remanded to John's care in John 19:26-27.

2.   A sister mentioned in 2 John:13.

3.   Her mentioned in Acts 1:14.

In the end, we must accept the facts that:

1.   While we feel pretty certain about to whom the letter was originally written, it has applied to millions of believers down through the centuries.

2.   It certainly fits the description of Scripture as we see in 2 Timothy 3:16-17.

3.   It applies to us today regardless of to whom it was originally addressed.

Reread: 2 John: 2

Why does John say he wrote the letter?

What unique privilege do all believers have by the power of the Holy Spirit?

See John 14:26 as you construct your answer.

How do you see this happening in practical every day terms?

In some ways, this echoes Pilate's cynical question to Jesus as we see in John 18:38.

We see the very important Biblical application of this in:

John 14:6.

John 1:1-3.

John 1:14.

John 10:10.

John 10:14.

John 10:30.

Isaiah 65:16.

John 8:32.

John 15:26.

Reread: 2 John:3

What three important things did John say would uniquely be with believers?

    1.

    2.

    3.

Note: Grace is often thought of as not deserving what you get. Conversely, mercy is thought of as not getting what you deserve.

Where do these things come from?

Be sure to access John 16:33 as you construct your answer.

For how long will these things be with those who have trusted Jesus Christ?

What two additional characteristics does John say will be evident in the lives of believers?

    1.

    2.

What do you think he means by this?

Reread: 2 John:4

What gave John great joy and happiness?

How might you define the difference between joy and happiness?

Note:

Joy is one of the fruits of the Spirit as seen in Galatians 5:22-23 most correctly considered to be welling up from within a person.

Happiness is most often thought of as relating to external circumstances or actions as experienced by a person.

Why do you think John had joy as a result of what he saw and heard?

Why do you think John had happiness as a result of meeting these people?

When have you seen other believers walking in the truth and finding great joy in it? Please explain.

Reread: 2 John:5

Also read: John 13:34

What command did John remind his readers of?

Why do you think he was reminding these people of the command at this point in time?

How should believers show love for one another?

Read 1 Corinthians 13 as you think about and discuss your answer.

Dr. Charles Missler said real love is a choice, not an emotion. What do you think of his statement?

Read: John 13:35

What is the result of believers showing this kind of love for each other?

Reread: 2 John:6

What two components did John say were implicit in real love for one another?

1.

2.

Why do you think that obeying the clear directives of Scripture is so endemic to love?

Reread: 2 John:7

What or whom did John say had gone out into the world?

What was the foundational component of what these deceivers were teaching?

Note: As we saw earlier, the teaching that Jesus Christ was more of a phantom was inherent in the false doctrines promulgated by the Gnostics. They claimed that Jesus did not even have a footprint. This is a good example of the misuse of Scripture. By taking a few verses out of context (See Matthew 14:25, Mark 6:48, and John 6:19) they arrived at this ridiculous conclusion that is so obviously in direct contradiction to the rest of God's Word.

Note 2: As we have said before, please remember the concepts in *How to Avoid Error* in the appendices of this book.

Why do you think it is so important that believers recognize the lies of the deceivers and hold on to the truth?

Please read the following verses as you think about and discuss your answer.

John 3:16

Ephesians 2:8-9

Galatians 1:4

Romans 10:9-10

Ephesians 4:17-30

Ephesians 5:11-16

Colossians 1:9-10

Reread: 2 John:8

What did John warn his readers against?

What did he encourage them to achieve?

Note: Scripture also speaks of rewards in terms of crowns. Please review the information below on crowns beginning in the last book of the Bible.

Crowns

The term used for crown in Revelation 2:10 is the Greek word *stephanos*. This is different that the crown one might find on royalty, referred to as a *diadem* in Greek. The priests of the various deities in Smyrna were termed *stephanophori* in reference to the laurel or golden crowns which they used to wear in public procession. They were awarded this honor at the end of their term in office. A *stephanos* was a crown of competed accomplishment. There are many crowns mentioned in Scripture and likely more than we are aware of.

Some of the crowns we are quite clear about are listed below. Take a look at the scripture references to obtain an understanding of each. These crowns are rewards for works. They are awarded by Jesus Christ Himself at the "Bema" or judgment seat in the future. Be sure to identify who might receive each crown listed expanding upon what is summarized after each.

1.   **Crown of Life.** See James 1:12 and Revelation 2:10.

    • For those who have suffered and endured for His sake.

2. **Crown of Righteousness.** See 2 Timothy 4:7-8.

   • For those who have fought the good fight, remained faithful and look eagerly forward to His appearing.

3. **Crown of Glory.** See 1 Peter 5:2-4.

   • For those who care for and watch over His flock.

4. **Crown of Incorruptibility.** See 1 Corinthians 9:24-25.

   • For those who steadfastly press on.

5. **Crown of Rejoicing.** See 1 Thessalonians 2:19-20.

   • For those who win souls.

Read: Matthew 25:21

Which of the crowns mentioned above will you win?

Reread: 2 John:9

What did those who denied then or today that Jesus Christ came in a real body indicate in a de-facto fashion?

Why do you think this is so?

Read the following verses as you construct your answer and realize sound Biblical truth.

Leviticus 17:11

Hebrews 9:22

Hebrews 2:14

Hebrews 9:12

Hebrews 9:14

1 John 2:2

John 1:17

John 3:16

Romans 5:9

1 Peter 1:18-19

Matthew 26:28

Revelation 5:9

In a similar way, what does it indicate when someone is true to the clear teaching of Scripture, which we call the Old and New Testaments?

Reread: 2 John:10

How did John say the people to whom he was writing should respond to false teachers?

   1.

   2.

What does it mean to not welcome a person who does not share in the teaching of Christ in practical terms?

Reread: 2 John:11

What happens to people who encourage false teachers?

How would welcoming a person with honor who purposely does not share in the correct teaching of Christ and God's Word share in their wickedness?

Why is this such a negative thing?

Note: See *How to Avoid Error* in the appendices of this book for further insight into how we can do this.

How can we avoid false teachers without being cold or inhospitable?

What sort of people should you deny a welcome into your home?

Reread: 2 John:12

Why did John not write down all he wanted to communicate?

What did he say would be the result of meeting his readers face to face?

Why do you think this would be so?

Reread: 2 John:13

Who did John say joined him in sending their greetings?

Note: This verse again relates back to the controversy sometimes heard about the recipient of this letter. For those to whom this has interest, Mary did indeed have a sister as noted in John 19:25. Whether this referred to her or to a group of believers is inconsequential to the import and power of this portion of Scripture. Believers will, at a future point, understand this with full clarity as we know from 1 Corinthians 13:12.

Application Questions

What specific steps can you take this coming week to demonstrate your caring and love for other believers?

What can you do today to be certain your life, attitudes, speech and practices are consistent with the clear truths of Scripture?

Close in Prayer

THE WORD OF LIFE
1 JOHN 1:1-4

Open in Prayer

Introduction to 1 John

1 John has often been called the sanctum sanctorum of the New Testament. It gives believers great insight into their relationship with God as His Child. In addition, it gives believers insight and instructions about their relationship with other members of God's family. As such, it has often proven to be of more importance to the day-to-day life of a believer than all of the other New Testament letters combined. (We do not herein pretend to say that any part of God's Word is unimportant or of less importance. We do, however, mean to say that certain portions are of particular help to believers as they relate to various things in everyday life.)

We need to pay attention to what God has graciously communicated to us through Scripture.

As we said at the outset of this book, life is real. It is not a playground or a simple preparation for the future. It is now, it is important, and everything within it has meaning.

Group Warm-Up Questions

What do you think of when you hear the term "fellowship"?

How do we know the events we read about in the history books really happened?

Note: The Bible is the most accurate book in existence when it speaks of matters of history. Archaeology, and indeed all other sciences, always confirm Scripture. A detailed study of this is most interesting, awe inspiring, and faith affirming. For more information on this, please see the appendices of this book paying particular attention to *Composite Probability* as well as *Science and History Confirm Scripture*.

Read: 1 John 1:1-4

Reread: 1 John 1:1

References to Jesus as the Word as well as to the Word of Life are intertwined. Please read the following scriptures and discuss what they mean.

Philippians 2:16

Hebrews 4:12

John 6:63

John 6:27

John 17:17

Isaiah 55:1-2

Jeremiah 15:16

Luke 4:4

Deuteronomy 8:3

John 1:1-3

John 5:39

Matthew 5:17

Ephesians 5:25-26

Please read 1 John 1:1 again.

What has existed from the beginning?

Who is called the Word of Life?

Who do you think made up the community of believers to whom John was referring? (Those to whom he was writing, those with him, or some combination of both.)

Why?

What contact did John, and the community of believers to which he was referring, have with the Word of Life?

Why do you think John stressed the personal, physical and historical interaction with Jesus that he and those to whom he was referring had with the Word of Life?

How important are firsthand eyewitness testimonies, such as John's, to your trust in Jesus?

How important are such eyewitness testimonies to people in the world today as they are confronted and presented with the claims of Jesus?

What personal testimony or witness do you have, and how do non-believers respond when they are faced with it?

Please think of some examples.

Is there anything that even approaches the importance of the Good News of Jesus Christ that you can share with others?

Reread: 1 John 1:2

How did God reveal himself to these people?

What did these believers proclaim about the Word of Life?

    1.

    2.

    3.

    4.

    5.

Is there anything in the world of greater importance than understanding these facts?

Given some of the heresies facing the early believers, especially that of Gnosticism which rose its head then and continues to do so today, why were the things John was proclaiming so important?

Reread: 1 John 1:3

What special characteristic of these people's proclamation was special and unique in an historical sense?

How do you think your witness would be impacted if you had seen and heard Jesus Christ Himself in physical form?

Why were John and those with him making the proclamations we are discussing?

Why do you think they wanted other believers to have fellowship with them?

Whose fellowship did John and those joining him in sending this letter enjoy?

What fellowship do you have with the Father and His Son, Jesus Christ?

What fellowship do you have with other believers?

How is our fellowship with God related to our fellowship with other believers?

What kinds of things can interfere with our fellowship with God and others?

Reread: 1 John 1:4

Why was this letter written?

In what ways can we enhance our fellowship?

In what way is your joy complete and how can you make sure you experience it on an ongoing basis?

Application Questions

What can you do to gain a better understanding and appreciation of the historical and scientific foundations of your faith?

What steps will you take this week to deepen your fellowship with other believers?

Close in Prayer

WEEK 4

WALKING IN THE LIGHT
1 JOHN 1:5-2:14

Open in Prayer

Group Warm-Up Questions

Why is it sometimes hard for someone to admit they were wrong about something?

About what kinds of things do people often tend to deceive themselves?

Read: 1 John 1:5-2:14

Reread: 1 John 1:5

From whom did John receive the message he was declaring?

What was this message?

Reread: 1 John 1:6

Is a person practicing the truth if they claim to have fellowship with God and yet live in spiritual darkness?

How so?

How would you characterize someone living in spiritual darkness?

What things might you see in the life of someone living in such darkness?

Please read the following verses and make a list of the prima facie evidences we might see in such a circumstance.

Romans 2:8

2 Thessalonians 2:12

Acts 26:26-27

Matthew 13:13

2 Peter 3:3

Proverbs 21:24

Jude 18

Isaiah 37:23

1 Corinthians 1:18

Psalm 14:1

Matthew 7:26

John 12:48

John 12:46

John 14:17

Romans 8:8-9

1 John 2:15-16

Ephesians 5:8-14

Galatians 5:19-21

1.

2.

3.

4.

5.

6.

Reread: 1 John 1:7

How might you define living in the light?

Read the following verses as you think about your answer.

2 Corinthians 4:6

John 14:15-17

Romans 8:8-9

John 5:26

John 5:21

John 6:40

John 6:57

John 14:6

John 1:4

John 8:12

John 12:46

Matthew 5:14-16

Ephesians 5:8-14

1 Thessalonians 5:5-6

Colossians 3:4

Galatians 5:22-25

What are the two ultimate and primary results of living in the light?

    1.

    2.

Why are these two things of such great importance?

Read 1 John 5:12 as you think about your answer.

Reread: 1 John 1:8

What is a person doing if they claim they have no sin and have achieved the perfection of God?

    1.

    2.

Reread: 1 John 1:9

Also read:

Romans 3:23

Romans 6:23

Romans 12:2

1 Corinthians 10:13

What happens if we confess our sins to God and ask His forgiveness and power to live as He desires?

What happens when we take part in this process?

Read John 10:10 as you think about your answer.

How do you feel about the promise of being cleansed of your sin and the new life available through Jesus Christ and the power of the Holy Spirit?

Please read the following verses as you contemplate your answer.

2 Timothy 1:7

Ephesians 3:16

Galatians 5:22-23

Reread: 1 John 1:10

What two things is someone actually doing if they claim they have not sinned?

     1.

     2.

Why might someone claim that they have no sin?

What role does confession of sins play in your daily life?

Reread: 1 John 2:1

What was John's purpose in writing this letter?

What advantage does a person have if they sincerely confess their sin and turn in the direction God desires as is evident in His Word?

2 Corinthians 5:17

2 Tim 3:16-17

What one and only one person in the history of the world is and always has been truly righteous?

1 Peter 2:22

Isaiah 53:9

Romans 5:12

1 John 2:29

Romans 5:1

Deuteronomy 32:4

In what way does Jesus act like our attorney?

Reread: 1 John 2:2

What did Jesus do for us?

To whom is this atoning sacrifice available?

Reread: 1 John 2:3-6

How can we tell if we or anyone else truly knows God and is living in the Light as mentioned in these few verses?

1.

2.

Please read the following verses for more information on this.

John 13:35

Matthew 7:15-20

How can we get to know God better?

Note: Sometimes one hears a person claiming that to say someone is not living a godly life is wrong. They say that the person making such a pronouncement is judging the person in question and that this is wrong. They often cite Matthew 7:1-3 as proof of this. However, such a person is utilizing one verse theology, which we must never do. (See *How to Avoid Error* in the appendices.)

We see how we are to apply God's standards in maintaining the order and clarity of purpose in our group in the following verses.

Let's take a look at what the whole of Scripture has to say about this.

Reread: 1 Timothy 1:19

What two primary directives did Paul give Timothy?

1.

2.

Does this also apply to us today? How so?

This verse says that some people have deliberately violated their consciences. How might they have done this?

What is the significance of the Scripture telling us that this violation of their consciences was "deliberate"?

Why is it so important that we realize this violation was an overt action of the will of these people?

What was the result when these people violated their consciences?

What do you take this to mean?

What happens when people do this today? Please think of an example and discuss:
1.   What it means for the people who do this.
2.   What it means for the community of believers with whom they are associated.
3.   How it impacts the non-believers who are always observing the lives of believers.

Read: Philippians 4:8

This verse taken in concert with 1 Timothy 1:19 infers that clinging to one's faith in Jesus and keeping one's conscience clear is also a matter of the will. What are your thoughts about this?

Reread: 1 Timothy 1:20

What two examples did Paul give of people who violated their consciences?

What two actions did Paul take when these people made such a negative choice?

Note: In this type of instance, it appears that the type of people in question have made an overt decision to go beyond the remedies available to them as referenced in:

James 5:16.

Romans 12:2.

Read:

Proverbs 13:20

Proverbs 14:7

Proverbs 25:26

Psalm 1:1-4

Psalm 119:115

Psalm 26:4-5

1 Corinthians 5:11-13

1 Corinthians 5:13

2 Corinthians 6:14

2 Peter 3:17

Numbers 16:1-35

How should we respond today when people in a group of believers also make such negative choices?

If we respond in accordance with Scripture as Paul did, what impact does it have upon the faithful believers in the group?

How does it impact a group of believers if we respond in direct contradiction to the Scriptures in a disobedient and weak-minded fashion, allowing these people to remain as active participants, treating them as legitimate and faithful followers?

How does it impact the effectiveness of the group if these people who have violated and continue to violate their consciences are seen by nonbelievers as representatives of what it means to be followers of Jesus?

Please discuss examples of when you have seen this handled in both ways and the impact it had.

Read:

Colossians 3:23-24

Colossians 4:5-6

Ephesians 4:29-30

What further light do these verses shed upon this subject?

What areas of your life do you need to examine more closely to determine to what extent you are living in concert with the Word of God?

Reread: 1 John 2:5

What is the litmus test that shows the degree to which we are living in Him?

Why is this concept so vitally important?

What happens if we fail this test?

Reread: 1 John 2:6-8

What did John say he was giving his readers?

What did John say was happening as believers came to have fellowship with God through Jesus Christ?

How important is fellowship in the life of a believer?

How should a believer act when placed in a situation where there are no other believers with whom to have fellowship?

Please read Colossians 4:4-6 and Daniel 12:3 as you construct your answer?

What does the way we treat fellow believers reveal about us?

Reread: 1 John 2:9

What does it indicate if someone claiming to be a believer hates a fellow believer?

1 John 2:10

What does not happen when believers have proper and positive relationships with one another?

Reread: 1 John 2:11

What are three characteristics of a believer who hates fellow believers?

    1.

    2.

    3.

Reread: 1 John 2:12

Why was John writing to this group of believers?

Read: Romans 8:28

What confidence should our relationship with God give us?

Reread: 1 John 2:13

Why was John writing to those mature in the faith?

Why was he writing to those young in the faith?

Reread: 1 John 2:14

What additional reason was John writing to this group of believers?

Why was this so important?

What additional reason was John writing to those who were mature in the faith?

Why was this so important?

What additional reasons was John writing to those young in the faith?

1.

2.

3.

Why was this so important?

How do you need to improve the way you deal with fellow believers in order to develop a deeper relationship with God?

Why is it that developing a Scripturally consistent and better relationship with other believers enhances our relationship with God?

Application Questions

What steps will you take this week to be sure you are walking in the light?

What will you do to incorporate honest self-evaluation and confession of any actions, thoughts, or attitudes that are not in line with God's Word into your daily routine?

Close in Prayer

WEEK 5

DO NOT LOVE THIS WORLD
1 JOHN 2:15-17

Open in Prayer

Group Warm-Up Questions

What makes TV commercials and advertisements so appealing?

What kinds of promises do TV commercials make?

Read: 1 John 2:15-17

Reread: 1 John 2:15

How do we love the world and the things in it?

What restrictions should we place on our affections?

What specific things should believers not love?

Please make a list.

1.

2.

3.

4.

5.

6.

7.

8.

9.

10.

Also read: 1 Timothy 6:9

What happens when people essentially make riches their god?

How can this subtly happen to even believers if they are not careful to be diligent in maintaining and growing in their relationship to God and other believers as well?

What is the result of loving the world?

If loving the world can interfere with one's relationship with God, what can we do to keep things in the proper perspective?

Reread: 1 John 2:16

What things does John list as being offered by the world, but not being of God?

    1.

    2.

    3.

    4.

Why do you think John categorized the things offered by the world as he did?

Please discuss each one of the four mentioned and enumerated above separately and why they can become a problem.

What things in the world are you tempted to love?

Why are the things of the world sometimes so enticing to us?

What things of the world do people substitute for God?

How can what we purposely see through our eyes help or harm us?

Please read Psalm 119:37 as you think about your answer.

How can our achievements be used for God's glory?

Read: Colossians 3:23-24 as you construct your answer.

Many years ago I was privileged to serve on the National Staff of the Fellowship of Christian Athletes with Paul Anderson. While Paul's name may have passed into history and may be unfamiliar to many people today, you can find him listed in the Guinness Book of World Records as the *world's strongest man.* He lifted 6,270 pounds off railroad trestles to claim this title. After winning the Olympics Paul had two great skills. One was, of course, weight lifting. There was little pecuniary gain in this.

His other skill was public speaking and the ability to share his faith both to a crowd and in writing. He authored several books and wrote a newspaper column that gained wide readership because of his athletic fame. He also started a home for delinquent boys still in operation today. When speaking he almost always said, "I am a national champion, a world champion and an Olympic champion, but the greatest thrill in my life is to know Jesus Christ."

Paul used his accomplishments and pedestal to great advantage for the Kingdom of God.

How can our possessions be used for God's glory?

Read the following verses as you think about your answer.

Genesis 14:19-20

Deuteronomy 14:22-23

2 Chronicles 31:4-5

Malachi 3:11-12

Malachi 1:12-13

Exodus 36:3-6

Proverbs 3:9-10

Ezra 2:68-69

Deuteronomy 16:17

Hebrews 7:1

Matthew 5:17

Matthew 5:23-24

Mathew 23:23

Luke 11:42

2 Corinthians 8:7

2 Corinthians 9:6-13

Matthew 6:19-21

Romans 12:13

Matthew 25:35-40

It is of interest that most people who call themselves Christians don't tithe today. According to *State of the Plate* only about ten to twenty-five percent of church members tithe. In fact, it is said that only five percent of the population participates in tithing. The average person claiming Christian affiliation today contributes only about 2.5% of their income. Looking back about one hundred years to the most difficult time the United States faced economically, which we call the Great Depression, those calling themselves Christians reportedly gave more. It is said that they averaged 3.3% of their income.

How do you account for this difference and the low rate of tithing among those calling themselves Christians both in the past and today?

Could it be that some of those calling themselves Christians were only so nominally or not at all?

Read the following verses and discuss what some of God's Word has to say about this subject.

Matthew 6:27-31

Matthew 6:33-34

1 Timothy 6:6-8

1 Timothy 6:17-19

Reread: 1 John 2:17

Also read:

John 15:18-20.

John 17:11.

John 17:14-15.

John 17:18.

Romans 12:2.

How can believers walk the tightrope of being in the world but not of it?

Should we be so sure of our position and commitment that the world and what it offers are things we can use and enjoy, but ultimately of little consequence. How so?

Please also read the following verses.

Hebrews 11:13

Hebrews 13:14

2 Corinthians 4:8-18

What does it mean to please God or to do the will of God as we see it in this verse?

God's Word provides us with clarity on doing His will.

Please read the following verses and discuss them together.

Ephesians 5:17

Colossians 1:9

Psalm 25:4-5

Psalm 25:8-9

Psalm 119:105

Proverbs 3:5-6

Proverbs 19:21

Jeremiah 29:10-14

Matthew 6:33

John 10:3-4

Romans 8:14

Romans 12:2

Ephesians 5:15-20

Philippians 2:12-13

1 Thessalonians 4:3-5

1 Timothy 2:3-4

Hebrews 10:35-36

Hebrews 13:20-21

What passes away?

Who or what lasts forever?

Who lives forever?

What is of lasting value?

From what worldly thing or value do you need to turn in order to properly pursue your relationship with God?

Read: John 17:18

Jim Elliot the famous martyred missionary said that a person is no fool who gives up what he cannot keep to gain what he cannot lose.

My friend Larry Norman, called *the Father of Christian Rock*, once said prior to his death that this world was not his home; he was just passing through.

Over one hundred years ago C. T. Studd famously wrote: "Only one life, twill soon be passed. Only what's done for Christ will last."

How does what these three believers said impact the way you think about your life, your thoughts, your speech, your actions, and how you spend your time?

Application Questions

What specific steps will you take to find satisfaction in your relationship with God rather than in the things of the world?

How will you do the will of God today?

Close in Prayer

WEEK 6

BEWARE THE ANTICHRISTS
1 JOHN 2:18-27

Open in Prayer

Group Warm-Up Questions

Who are the enemies of believers today?

What do you think is the best defense against cults and other false spiritual teaching?

What effect do you think warning labels on cigarettes and alcohol have?

Read: 1 John 2:18-27

Introductory Groundwork

Today we are examining material dealing with the first time the words *Antichrist* and *antichrists* are used in Scripture. It will come as a surprise to many that these words are used only five times in the whole of the Bible and those five times are all in the books we call First and Second John.

To use a popular phrase in today's popular semantics, what's up with that?

Excellent Question.

Most people think the Antichrist is a central figure, primarily in the book of Revelation and are completely nonplussed when they hear the term *antichrists*, thinking it is a misprint.

In fact, many people in history have wondered if some personage they consider dastardly might indeed be the Antichrist they imagine to be mentioned in Revelation and predicted in the Old Testament. We have seen such disparate people as Napoleon, Adolf Hitler, Putin, Rasputin, Saddam Hussein, Barack Obama, and Donald Trump all mentioned as possibly being THE Antichrist. Of course, everyone making such an assumption has been wrong.

It is of some note that the term *Antichrist* is mentioned in only one place in the Bible, and that is in 1 John 2:18. This personage is mentioned by that very popular name in this place alone, but by many other descriptive names throughout Scripture. We see him called the *Man of Sin*, the *Man of Lawlessness* in 2 Thessalonians 2:3-12, the *Man of Desolation* in Matthew 24:15, the *Sacrilegious Object that Causes Desecration* in Mark 13:14, *The Prince That Shall Come* in Daniel 7:24-27, the *Deceiver* in 2 John 7, and the *Beast* in Revelation 13:1-10.

The commonality among all of these descriptions is that this personage comes in what the Bible calls the *last hour*, is a liar, is one way or another referred to as a deceiver, and most certainly operates in opposition to Jesus Christ. This subject is dealt with in great detail in Dave Hunt's book *A Woman Rides the Beast* as well as in Chuck Missler's various series on *Revelation*, *The Four Horsemen of the Apocalypse*, *The Church in the End Times*, *End Times Scenario*, *The Magog Invasion*, *The Next Holocaust* and more. Dr. Missler and Dr. Masten also collaborated on a fine summary in *Expectations of the Antichrist*. The material from Chuck Missler is some of the best ever produced and is available from Koinonia House and can be found at Khouse.org.

What about the plural of the word presented as *antichrists* you may ask. This obviously refers to a group of people and while generally described in Scripture refers to people with certain characteristics. We may, in fact, see many such people today and most certainly will see them in the future according to God's Word itself. These people have several common characteristics most often including some or all of the following:

1. They have gone out from or divorced themselves from the mainstream church or body of sincere believers who adhere to the clear teachings of Scripture.

2. They are a threat to the community of believers often called *the Church*.

3. One way or another they deny that Jesus is the Christ.

4. They deny that Jesus came from God.

5. They are not faithful to Scripture.

6. They quite obviously do not have the indwelling power of the Holy Spirit.

7. They deny that Jesus came in the flesh. (Often in the same way as the Gnostics. This old group is still around, but under cloaks of different names.)

Reread: 1 John 2:18-27

Reread: 1 John 2:18

What time did John say it is?

What makes you think we are living in the last hour today?

Who did he say was coming and who did he say had come at this time?

Reread: 1 John 2:19

Where did these antichrists come from?

Why did they leave?

What did they prove by leaving?

What antichrists are active in the world today?

Reread: 1 John 2:20

What did the believers to whom John was writing have?

What did the believers to whom John was writing know?

How would you describe the truths we know about Christ?

Reread: 1 John 2:21

What important differentiation were the believers to whom John was writing able to make?

Note: When bank, secret service, law enforcement, or treasury employees are taught to recognize counterfeit currency they are trained by intensive study of the real thing. They know what it looks like, what color it is, how things are positioned on it, the inherent contrast on it, the paper it is printed on, the feel of it, the exact size of it and just about anything else we might think of. When someone presents them with a phony dollar bill, they don't need to study it. They know as soon as they see it.

Some counterfeiters are very skillful, but a properly trained person won't be fooled. They know the real thing.

Why then, do you think the people to whom John was writing could not be fooled when someone made false claims about God's Word or Jesus Christ?

How can we be sure to be in such a position?

Reread: 1 John 2:22

What are some of the ways the people John was writing to were told they could detect antichrists?

1.

2.

3.

4.

Reread: 1 John 2:23

In what way is denying or acknowledging the Son related to having the Father?

Reread: 1 John 2:24

What did John encourage his readers to do?

What did he tell them would be the result of this?

Reread: 1 John 2:25

What eternal, powerful and unmatchable privilege is accorded those who remain in fellowship with the Father and the Son?

Reread: 1 John 2:26

Why, in particular, was John writing to his readers about these things?

What groups of people are trying to lead people astray today?

Note: We should realize that our enemy is always trying to mislead or misdirect believers as we see in Matthew 24:24.

However, Scripture teaches us that we can be victorious over the efforts of antichrists with such an agenda.

Please read the following references and discuss what they mean to you.

1 John 5:4-5

Ephesians 1:4

1 Peter 1:5

Jude 1:1

John 10:2-5

Reread: 1 John 2:27

What did the Holy Spirit teach the believers to whom John was writing?

What does He teach believers today?

How can we protect ourselves against false teachers and antichrists?

How can we remain in fellowship with Jesus Christ?

What are some of the other results experienced by those who have received the Holy Spirit?

Read Galatians 5:22-23 as you construct your answer.

This however, is not the only thing we should know about the Holy Spirit. It does give us a good, but not quite complete picture. In fact, I am not sure if I or any other human being has this ability. However, thankfully God has given us a great deal of information about the Holy Spirit as we can see in the following material.

Role of the Holy Spirit in the Old and New Testament

Note: He is and has been continually active whether we realize it or not.

1. First, we should realize that the Holy Spirit and His role as part of the Trinity is nothing new. His role has been evident throughout history. As point in fact, we see that Jesus expected students of the Old Testament to understand this. We see this in:

- Genesis 1:2.

- Job 26:13.

- Isaiah 42:1-9.

- John 3:10.

- John 3:5-8.

2. The Holy Spirit convicts a person of sinful behavior and their need for Jesus Christ in their lives. We see this in:

    - John 16:8-11.

3. The Holy Spirit has a number of definable characteristics. We see this defined in Isaiah 11:2 as:

    - The Spirit of the LORD.

    - The Spirit of wisdom.

    - The Spirit of understanding.

    - The Spirit of counsel.

    - The Spirit of power and might.

    - The Spirit of knowledge.

    - The Spirit of the fear of the Lord.

4. We should also note that the apostle Paul as well as Ezekiel, Samuel and others clearly understood that the Holy Spirit inspired the Old and New Testament writers. We see this in:

- 2 Samuel 23:2.

- Ezekiel 2:2.

- 2 Timothy 3:16-17.

5.   The Holy Spirit inspired the writers of the Old Testament in such a way that they were able to accurately prophesy about the first and second coming of the Jewish Messiah as well as His impact on what is referred to as the Millennium. We see this in:

- Isaiah 11:1-5.

- Isaiah 61:1.

- Luke 4:18-19.

- Isaiah 61:2.

- Ezekiel 36:27.

6.   The Holy Spirit is involved in what the Scriptures call the circumcision of one's heart. We see this in:

- Deuteronomy 30:6.

- Ezekiel 11:19-20.

- Ezekiel 36:26-29.

- Jeremiah 4:4.

- Romans 12:2.

- Romans 2:25-29.

- 2 Corinthians 5:17.

7.   The result of the Holy Spirit's regenerating work is faith. We see this in:

- Ephesians 2:8.

- Hebrews 11:13.

- Hebrews 11 as a whole where we see that this faith was evidenced in the lives of those who trusted the One True God and looked forward to his Messiah.

8.   The Holy Spirit's indwelling in the Old Testament was generally selective and temporary, normally associated with short and sometimes long-term work. We see this in:

- Numbers 27:18.

- 1 Samuel 16:12-13.

- 1 Samuel 10:10.

- 1 Samuel 16:14

- Judges 3:10.

- Judges 6:34.

- Judges 13:25.

- Judges 14:6.

- Psalm 143:10.

- John 7:37-39.

9.   The Holy Spirit's indwelling in the New Testament is ongoing and produces definitive results. We see this in

- 1 Corinthians 3:16-17.

- 1 Corinthians 6:19-20.

- Galatians 5:22-23.

- 2 Timothy 1:7.

10. The Holy Spirit in the lives of believers acts as a restrainer of evil. This is clearly evident as New and Old Testament believers are to bring about good as a result of adhering to God's standards in their culture, society and times. We see this succinctly summarized in:

- 1 Kings 3:9-12.

- James 3:17.

- Colossians 4:5-6.

- Ephesians 4:29-30.

- Romans 12:2.

- Joshua 1:8.

- Amos 5:24.

- 2 Thessalonians 2:6-7.

11. The indwelling of believers in New Testament times, including ours, can quench the Holy Spirit and must allow Him reign in one's life as we see in:

- 1 Thessalonians 5:16-20.

12. The major differentiation between the New and Old Testament indwelling of the Holy Spirit is that in the New His indwelling is ongoing, although as noted above, it can be quenched if one is not careful and obedient. We see this ongoing characteristic in:

   • John 14:7

13. As noted at the beginning of this list, God also acts in and through history even if it is not apparent at the time. For a few examples of this we can see:

   • The utilization of Cyrus the Great by God to facilitate the return of the Jews to their homeland. We see this in prophecy and its fulfillment around 538 B.C. in:

     1. Isaiah 44:28-Isaiah 45:1-5 where God calls Cyrus by name 150 years before his birth.

     2. 2 Chronicles 36:22-23 where Cyrus decrees the release of the Jews to their homeland.

     3. Ezra 1:1-11 where Cyrus assists in the rebuilding of the temple and the restoration of the temple treasuries.

     4. Ezra 3:7 which mentions a number of the specific things Cyrus facilitated in the temple reconstruction.

     5. Ezra 4:4-5 where the rebuilding of the temple is also recorded.

   • The Battle of Thermopylae in 480 B.C. when 300 Greek Spartan warriors accompanied by 7,000 other Greek fighters fought off an invading Persian force stated in ancient literature as numbering in the millions. This facilitated the future spread of the Good News of Jesus Christ with the then future standardization and implementation utilizing the precision of the Greek language. (Writers in modern times sometimes have trouble believing that an ancient army could be as large as the Persians claim, thinking it could "only" have numbered 200,000 to 300,000. However, it is interesting to note that when modern historians have attempted to insert their own opinions and deride ancient documents, the ancient documents, even when not biblical, have tended to have the ring of truth when examined in an honest, archaeological, historical and analytical fashion.) As an interesting side note, the name of the Greek King who led 300 Spartans against the Persian horde was Leonidas. According to www. greek-names.info/leonidas/ Leonidas means lion. Most people who study the Bible and prophecy come to understand that there are no coincidences when it comes to God. It may, however, come as some surprise to many to realize that the heroic actions and sacrifice of the Spartan King Leonidas and his brave companions paved the way for the spread of the Good News about Jesus Christ. Jesus Christ Himself is sometimes also referred to as The Great Lion of Judah in Scripture. (See Genesis 49:10, Isaiah 31:4, Hosea 13:7-8, and Revelation 5:5.)

- Another return of the Jews to their homeland in the 20th century as prophesied in the Old Testament and accomplished on May 14, 1948 and unwittingly facilitated by Adolf Hitler.

Note: By this time, you may have noticed that the gift of tongues, as it is herein referred is not included on the above list. This is not to say that it is unimportant or that some believers do not have an experience of this nature in accord within Scriptural parameters. However, it would appear that the other manifestations of the Holy Spirit are more far-reaching and evident universally in the lives of believers and in history itself.

We should note that the Apostle Paul spoke about this in depth in 1 Corinthians 14. There is a tendency in the world today to either put too little emphasis or too much emphasis on speaking in tongues and the work of the Holy Spirit. Our simple desire is to see this as God does and as evident in His Word.

One must approach this topic with a sound Scriptural base, a sound mind (2 Timothy 1:7), prayer and indeed the power of the Holy Spirit. Upon a more global study of such phenomena, we find a similar vocalization occurring in pagan cultures and religions that quite obviously have nothing at all to do with the Holy Spirit. This should come as no surprise as we view such texts as 2 Corinthians 11:14, 1 Peter 5:8 and again 2 Timothy 1:7.

Remember: The Holy Spirit always acts in concert with the Word of God. Any deviation from that standard claimed by someone is in fact a falsehood. See *How to Avoid Error* in the appendices of this book.

Application Questions

What will you do on an ongoing basis to be sure you know the truth of the Scriptures and Jesus Christ?

What specific steps will you take to better prepare yourself against antichrists in the world today and their false teachings?

Who is someone you can encourage in their growth as a believer this week so that they can better know the truth and stand up against attacks from the personage known in the Bible as the evil one?

Close in Prayer

WEEK 7

CHILDREN OF GOD
1 JOHN 2:28-3:10

Open in Prayer

Group Warm-Up Questions

In what way are you like your mother or father?

What was one of the benefits of being the child of your parents as you were growing up?

How would most people define the term "sin"?

Read: 1 John 2:28-3:10

Reread: 1 John 2:28

With whom did John encourage those to whom he was writing to stay in fellowship?

What does it mean for someone to continue in fellowship with Christ?

What did he say would be the result of this ongoing fellowship?

    1.

    2.

When did he say these things would be most evident?

Reread: 1 John 2:29

What is true about everyone who does what is right, using the Judeo-Christian Scriptures as the crucible to determine right and wrong?

Reread: 1 John 3:1

How has the father lavished love upon believers?

Why do people of the world not always recognize that believers are, in truth, God's children?

What further step must unbelievers take in order to recognize that those who have trusted Christ are God's children?

Reread: 1 John 3:2

Also Read:

John 1:12-13

Galatians 3:23

Galatians 3:26

1 John 5:1

Romans 8:14-17

What are believers now in a de-facto fashion whether or not they are recognized as such?

What has God not yet shown His children?

What has God shown believers about what they will be like?

When will this happen?

What is so great about being a child of God?

Reread: 1 John 3:3

Also read: 2 Timothy 2:21-26

What kind of person keeps themselves clean or pure?

Whose example and command are these people following?

How are you preparing yourself for the impending return of Jesus Christ?

Reread: 1 John 3:4

Also read: Romans 3:23

Who has sinned?

How would you define sin?

Who continues to overtly sin?

Reread: 1 John 3:5

Also read:

Ephesians 2:8-9

Romans 6:23

Hebrews 2:18

Hebrews 4:15-16

Why did Jesus come into the world as a human being?

What was the difference in how Jesus responded to temptation in comparison to every other human being, whether one admits it or not?

Read: 1 Corinthians 10:13

What ability and privilege Do believers have today?

Reread: 1 John 3:6

What is unusual about someone who lives in Christ?

Is there some kind of difference between overt and purposeful sin versus unintentional mistakes?

What is wrong with the statement heard in some denominations that "they (church members and supposed believers) sin every day and in every way"?

How would you describe a person who does not sin?

What difficulties arise when one takes 1 John 3:6 out of context as some denominations unfortunately do?

What is wrong with what many have called one verse theology?

(Please read and discuss *How to Avoid Error* in the appendices of this book.)

When have you seen a person try and live in concert with a single Biblical verse and what happened?

Reread: 1 John 3:7

What does it show when someone does "what is right" according to the Biblical definition?

Reread: 1 John 3:8

What does it show when someone continues making life choices in direct contradiction to the Biblical standard?

Who has been sinning since the beginning?

Read: John 3:16 and 1 John 3:8

For what reason did the Son of God come into the world?

How would you describe what the Scriptures mean when they say that the Son of God came into the world to "destroy the works of the devil"?

When have you seen this process taking place in the life of a believer?

Reread: 1 John 3:9

Also read:

Colossians 3:3

Galatians 3:26

Galatians 4:4-7

Romans 12:2

Why can't a person who has been born of God continue to habitually, overtly and purposefully sin?

Reread: 1 John 2:21

Also read:

1 John 2:1

2 Corinthians 5:21

Romans 8:15

Having read today's passage, how would you explain the fact that those who have trusted Jesus do sin with the statements that they cannot sin or keep sinning?

Reread: 1 John 3:10

Also read: 2 Corinthians 5:17

Romans 8:14

Matthew 5:43-48

What can we observe in the life of a person who has become a child of God?

How do they live?

Read: John 8:44

What do you observe in the life of a person who the Bible calls a child of the Devil?

How can we know that we are children of God in the terms of Scripture?

Do you need to change your daily routine so that you may be confident and unashamed before Christ at His second coming? How so?

If you are a believer, how have you felt when your unbelieving friends or acquaintances did not understand you?

Read: Matthew 5:10-13

How can we take joy and encouragement from this?

How can we use this differentiation as an opportunity to share our faith?

Application Questions

What steps will you take to keep yourself pure, even as the Jewish Messiah, Yeshua HaMaschiach, Jesus Christ, is pure.

What area of weakness will you ask God to strengthen this week?

Close in Prayer

LOVE ONE ANOTHER
1 JOHN 3:11-24

Open in Prayer

Group Warm-Up Questions

Who, in your opinion, is someone in history or alive today whose life was an example of what it means to love (exclusive of Jesus Christ)? Why?

Who, in your opinion, is someone in history or alive today whose life is an example of what it means to hate?

Read: 1 John 3:11-24

Also Read: John 13:34

What new command did Jesus Himself give his followers?

Before going further, we should briefly look at the original language of the text. In Greek there are several types of love. This is delineated by the Greek words:

Eros, which refers to the type of romantic or sexual attraction felt between two people. (*Eros* is the noun for this type of love. When expressed as a verb it appears as *eran.*)

Storge, which refers to the love felt between family members as in a parent and a child. (*Storge* is the noun for this type of love. When used as a verb it appears as *stergein.*)

Philia, which refers to "brotherly" love and is most often exhibited in a close friendship. (The noun for this type of love is *philia,* while the verb is *phileo.*)

Agape, which refers to the self-sacrificial type of deep love that might cause a person to lay down their life to save another person. (*Agape* is the noun form of this love and *agapeo* is the verb form.) There is no higher word for love in the Greek New Testament.

The Bible speaks specifically of *philia* and *agape. Eros* and *storge* do not expressly appear in the Bible, although the concepts are obviously there.

Reread: John 13:34

The Greek word used for love in John 13:34 is *agape.*

Reread: 1 John 3:11

What message had John's audience heard from the beginning?

Reread: 1 John 3:12

For what reasons did Cain kill his brother?

    1.

    2.

    3.

    4.

    5.

    6.

We would be remiss to assume that everyone today knows the story of Cain and the implications it has.

First, we would do well to remember what Jesus said about murders and liars.

Read John 8:44 and jot down what we learn.

Next, we should review the story of Cain on an historical basis by reading Genesis 4:1-16. Here we should note several things from the text that aid in our understanding:

    1.   Cain was not an atheist.

    2.   Instead, Cain is shown as an insincere worshiper of God who:

- Certainly, gave a portion of his crops, but apparently not really his best (Genesis 4:3).

- Harbored some sin in his life, the full extent of which we are unaware (Genesis 4:6-7).

- Did not really know God (1 John 4:8).

- Deceived his brother.

- Murdered his brother.

- Lied to God.

Reread: 1 John 3:13

About what should believers not be surprised?

Why is this sometimes such a shock to believers, especially new ones?

Why do believers sometimes receive such a response from those who have not found new life through the Son?

Have you ever experienced the hatred of the world? What happened?

Read John 15:18-25 to see what Jesus had to say about this. Please enumerate the key points that Jesus made in this passage.

1.

2.

3.

4.

5.

6.

7.

8.

9.

Conversely, why do unbelievers sometimes find themselves in a position where they admire, respect, want to emulate, and even want to possess what believers have been blessed to find?

Please read the following verses and discuss what is going on in situations like this.

Philippians 1:27

John 14:6

Matthew 5:16

1 Timothy 4:12

Colossians 4:5-6

Reread: 1 John 3:14

How can a believer discern if they have passed from death to life?

What does it mean for believers to love one another?

Do you ever struggle with loving other believers? How so?

What do we know about a person who has no love?

Reread: 1 John 3:15

What do we know about a person who hates a believing brother or sister even if they claim to know God?

What do we know about murderers or pseudo-believers who are actually mongers and purveyors of hate?

In what ways does love result in life?

In what ways does hate result in death?

Avi Lipkin, when serving in the Israeli military at the general's rank, said that when you hate someone you prepare a vial of poison for your adversary and then you drink it yourself. What do you think about his statement?

Reread: 1 John 3:16

How do we know what real love is?

How might we see this working out in daily life in times where the situation is not physical life or death?

Have you ever interceded for someone who was somehow at risk on a personal or professional level? What happened?

Do you think such intercession is more meaningful when one's life is on the line or when one's reputation is at stake? Please explain?

Reread: 1 John 3:17

What did John ask his readers?

Do you think this is a legitimate test of a believer's love for other believers? How so?

Read 2 Thessalonians 3:10

Why do believers sometimes struggle to have this in balance in accordance with the Word of God?

How does this relate to the old proverb about teaching a person to fish instead of giving them a fish? Please explain.

Do you ever struggle to love other people who call themselves Christians? How so?

How, in practical terms, do you demonstrate your love for fellow believers?

Why do those who call themselves Christians sometimes struggle with demonstrating their love for others with the use of "their" possessions?

If one is a believer, who is really the owner of their possessions? Read the following verses as you put your answer together.

Psalm 24:1

Psalm 50:10-12

Matthew 24:14-30

Reread: 1 John 3:18-19

Why is it easier to love with words rather than actions?

If believers love one another, what should be the practical result as observed on a daily basis?

What are some of the results of believers showing their love and concern for one another?

　　1.

　　2.

　　3.

　　4.

　　5.

Read: James 2:15-16

What does it indicate if our claimed love does not show itself in our actions?

Reread: 1 John 3:20

What is God greater than?

What does this mean to you?

What does God know?

How might you explain the concept of an infinitely knowledgeable supreme God to someone who has a finite mind?

Why might it be hard for someone with a finite mind to grasp the magnificence of God?

How would you explain the simultaneous arrogance and ignorance of someone who denies that God exists?

Read Romans 1:20-25 as you think about your answer?

Is there hope for such a person? Please read the following few verses and explain.

Ephesians 2:8-9

Romans 3:23

Romans 6:23

Romans 12:2

Reread: 1 John 3:21

What is the result in terms of one's feelings of realizing that their sin has been covered by the sacrificial shed blood of Jesus?

Reread: 1 John 3:22

What promise do we find in this verse?

What are the prerequisites for receiving the results of this promise?

How can we be sure to think and live in such a way that we might receive the results of this promise?

Please read the following verses as you construct your answer.

John 10:10

2 Timothy 3:16-17

Philippians 4:6-7

Philippians 4:8

Romans 12:2

Reread: 1 John 3:23

Also read: Romans 13:8-10

What are the two primary prerequisite components one must meet in order to please God?

How might you explain each of these components in Biblical terms to someone who is unfamiliar with them?

Reread: 1 John 3:24

What is the two-part result of obeying God's commandments?

1.

2.

Why must these two actions and attitudes be met to please God?

Why must these things be in place before one can experience the abundant life mentioned in John 10:10?

How can we know that God lives in us?

What should we evidence in our lives if the Holy Spirit lives in us? Read Galatians 5:22-23 as you put together your answer.

Can one use these two simple verses as a sort of basic crucible or personally administered test to be sure they are living, speaking and acting as God desires? How so?

Please give an example of how this might work in the life of a believer.

In what way does hate result in death?

How does the Biblical concept of Agape' love result in life?

Application Questions

For what fellow believer whom you have difficulty loving will you do something kind this week?

How can you use your material possessions to show love for another believer this week?

Close in Prayer

WEEK 9

TEST THE SPIRITS
1 JOHN 4:1-6

Open in Prayer

Group Warm-Up Questions

What standards would you use to test a person's credentials to do your job?

What credentials do you have to do your job?

What makes something either "worldly" or "Christian"?

Read: 1 John 4:1-6

What did John instruct his readers to do?

What did he instruct his readers to not do?

Who did John say had gone out into the world?

What spirits should we be testing today?

What false prophets are in the world today?

Obviously, this kind of almost double agent activity is not new. It has been going on for thousands of years and our enemy employs it with great success to the detriment and doom of its adherents.

Read:

Jude 4

2 Peter 2:1-3

Matthew 7:15

Matthew 24:11

Matthew 24:24

Where in today's culture have you seen such false prophets?

Dr. Charles Missler, one of the most intelligent, well-read, and prolific of the great Bible teachers of all time, said that many of these false prophets are today in the pulpits of churches.

What do you think about what Chuck said?

Overall, what segments of the world today would you say are controlled or influenced by the spirit of the antichrist?

Reread: 1 John 4:2

What is one of the primary ways that a person claiming to have the Spirit of God can be recognized?

Read:

Isaiah 7:14

Isaiah 9:6-7

Jeremiah 23:5

Matthew 1:18

Matthew 1:20

Matthew 1:21

Matthew 1:22

Matthew 1:23

Matthew 1:25

Matthew 1:18-25

Luke 2:21

Luke 1:34

Luke 1:36-38

John 1:14

Galatians 4:4

Micah 5:2

Luke 1:26-34

Luke 1:31

Luke 1:35

Luke 1:34-38

Colossians 1:15-17

1 Timothy 2:5

1 Corinthians 8:6

John 1:1

John 1:3

John 6:40-41

John 8:24

Luke 1:34-35

Matthew 1:22-23

Hebrews 1:2-3

Galatians 4:4-5

John 20:28

John 8:58

John 3:16-17

Revelation 1:13-18

Revelation 1:8

The virgin birth of Jesus Christ is not just important, **it is essential**. Having read the verses above, why might you say this is so?"

    1.

    2.

    3.

    4.

    5.

    6.

    7.

Reread: 1 John 4:2-3

How might you summarize in succinct fashion how we might recognize that someone most definitely is not representing the one true God or His Son?

Read: 2 Timothy 3:16-17

What is the sole source of incontrovertible revealed truth in written form as it pertains to all of life, including spiritual matters?

Since this is our source of truth, the enemy is well aware of it and tries to remove this weapon from the hands of believers. However, believers cannot allow this to happen and God has equipped them to stand up to the attempts of the enemy to disarm them.

Read and Discuss: *How to Avoid Error* in the Appendices of this book.

Since the truth of the Scriptures is paramount, please also review and discuss *Composite Probability Theory* in the Appendices of this book. For anyone who does not know it already, **it is absolutely empirically and statistically impossible for Jesus not to be who he claimed to be.**

Read 1 John 4:3

What spirit does not acknowledge that Jesus came from God?

Reread: 1 John 4:4

Why does the writer say that believers have overcome the spirit of the antichrist?

Besides the spirit of the antichrist, over who else have believers already won a victory even though the battle is not yet done?

Read: Revelation 17:14

If you have trusted Jesus Christ, you are on the winning side of this ongoing Cosmic battle. How do you feel about this?

How does it make you feel to know that if you are a believer, you have overcome the world in the present tense as well as in the future?

If you are a believer, how are you impacted by the knowledge that the Spirit that is within you is greater than the spirit of the world? Please make a list.

   1.

   2.

   3.

   4.

   5.

   6.

   7.

Reread: 1 John 4:5

From what viewpoint do those with the spirit of the antichrist speak?

Reread: 1 John 4:6

Who does not listen to those who belong to the Father, Son and the Holy Spirit?

Who does listen to those who belong to the Father, Son and Holy Spirit?

How can we recognize if someone has the Spirit of Truth?

How can we know if someone has the spirit of deception?

How would you distinguish between seeing from the world's viewpoint and seeing from God's viewpoint?

1.

2.

3.

4.

5.

6.

7.

How can we reflect our confidence in the supremacy of Jesus Christ in everyday living?

As we complete today's study, we should also review Ephesians 6:10-18 to be sure we have each availed ourselves of the equipment essential to winning the victory in our lives. This is famously called the *Armor of God.*

Application Questions

What influences in your life (such as books, magazines, music, ideas, podcasts, television shows) will you put to the test this week to see if they are from God?

What false prophets do you need to guard yourself against this week?

Close in Prayer

GOD'S LOVE AND OUR LOVE
1 JOHN 4:7-21

Open in Prayer

Introductory Notes:

As we noted early on in the study of 1 John, this book of the Bible is in many ways the ***sanctus santorum*** of the New Testament. It goes to the heart of one's faith in deep and descriptive principles that we must all learn if we are to live the victorious lives God makes available to us through Jesus and the Holy Spirit. In this study and the next, God has outlined the true nature of real love for us. With each of the seven points of love as delineated in 1 John we also see details to assist us in realizing it in our lives in practical terms.

As a preface and aid to this section of Scripture I am herein presenting a preliminary outline with general references so that we know what to expect. This is then followed with a detailed investigation into the component parts as noted.

The Seven Points of Real Love

Three Foundational Facts

1. God is Love.

    • This is seen in 1 John 4:7-8.

2. God demonstrated His love by sending His Son.

    • This is seen in 1 John 4:9-11.

3. God continues to show His love by the indwelling of the Holy Spirit.

    • This is seen in 1 John 4:12-16.

Four Evidences of God's Love as Believers are Perfected

4. The confidence a believer can know in His relationship with God.

    • This is seen in 1 John 4:17-19.

5. The honesty of God's love in the life of a believer.

    • This is seen in 1 John 4:20-21.

6. The joyful obedience in daily living a believer experiences.

    • This is seen in 1 John 5:1-3.

7. The victory over the world each believer has through the Father, Son and Holy Spirit.

    • This is seen in 1 John 5:4-5.

We interrupt this program: When writing this chapter, I was in Pennsylvania for a week of in-person work. It was President's Day so I was at our house in Pittsburgh working on the text. I received a call at about 9:30 a.m. and from caller ID thought it was from my good friend, Bill. But it wasn't Bill. It was his wife in tears telling me that Bill had just had a stroke and passed away. Bill was one of the top tax attorneys in the United States and we enjoyed both a professional and personal association for the better part of 5 decades. I mention this here as this interruption in my preparation caused me to not only pray for Bill's family and to give thanks for him, but to also carefully review the Scriptural truths in this lesson. We would all do well to not only take these vital truths to heart, but to also realize that we know not the day nor the hour of our passing and we must always be ready for this impending event.

Further Information on Numbers in Scripture

Jesus uses the phrase "verily, verily" (KJV and YLT), "most assuredly" (NKJV), "I Tell you the truth" (NIV84 and NLT) seven times in the book of John. When He does this, He seems to be making a point of great emphasis. He is not just saying that something is true and important, but that it is really important that we should pay attention to it. The seven places in the book of John that Jesus uses this language with the quote involved are:

1. John 6:48 "I AM the bread of life."

2. John 8:12 "I AM the light of the world."

3. John 10:9 "I AM the door."

4. John 10:11 "I AM the good shepherd."

5. John 11:25 "I AM the resurrection and the life."

6.   John 14:6 "I AM the way, the truth and the life."

7.   John 15:1 "I AM the true vine."

Besides serving as direct statements about the role of Jesus, there appears to be even more at work here.

If we take a look at Exodus 3:13-15 we find that Jesus is also affirming His deity with these seven "I AM" statements in John.

By now, particularly in the writings of John, we have seen that numbers in scripture seem to have some significance. This should not be too surprising to us since we know that everything in the Word of God is there by design. This includes every detail, every place name, and indeed the structure of the documents themselves.

Each of the "I AM" statements in the Gospel of John is found in the context of one of seven key discourses in the book. And, when reviewed in depth, it appears that each of these discourses in some way mirrors the past, present and future as it relates to Israel.

So what does this tell us? If nothing else, the recurrence of such constructs in the structure of Scripture shows that it is of supernatural origin. No human being could put together a book like the Bible with such structural and even numerical interrelatedness throughout. We need to again stand in awe of this book that God had provided to us.

When thinking about the number seven, many commentators have said that it is the number of divinity or perfection. However, a large number of respected scholars, including Dr. Charles Missler, say that a more correct understanding is that seven is the number of completeness. This makes sense, especially when we see how it is used in relationship to Jesus, God, Israel, history and Scripture as a whole. When we see the number seven also involved with the enemy of God in Revelation 12:3, Dr. Missler's point seems quite well taken. The enemy of God and his work can be complete in a negative sense, while the number seven can also delineate completeness in a positive sense in relationship to the Lord and His plan.

So again, where does this leave us? It leaves us with a sense of awe and appreciation for the Word of God. It can be trusted above all else.

Those interested in reading more about this topic might find the book *Number in Scripture: Its Supernatural Design and Spiritual Significance* by E. W. Bullinger of interest. This in-depth study of what is called gematria is fascinating. The book description on Amazon refers to it as "an invaluable guide to the study of Bible Numerics. Its two-fold approach to the subject first examines the supernatural design of the Bible and its' amazing patterns of numbers and numerical features of the scriptures that give evidence of their designer. The second section highlights the spiritual significance and symbolic connotations of numbers which are repeated in different contexts throughout the Bible. The study will provide a treasure of insights and practical applications for pastors, teachers and Bible students.

When we realize that this book was written in 1894 without the benefit of a computer, we gain a greater appreciation for the burning intelligence and scholarship of the author. E. W. Bullinger (1837-1913) was a direct descendant of Johann H. Bullinger, the Swiss reformer. Bullinger was a lifelong scholar and writer studying at King's College, London. In 1862 he was ordained in the Church of England. He is the author of the notes and appendixes of *The Companion Bible* and the author of numerous works including *Commentary on Revelation*, *Great Cloud of Witnesses*, *How to Enjoy the Bible*, and *Number in Scripture*.

While this is wonderful, fascinating, and inspiring work, one must still approach it and all similar matters with a note of caution. The writer of Hebrews cautions us in the NKJV by saying in Hebrews 13:9, "Do not be carried about with various and strange doctrines." Our faith is founded on the Word of God and rooted in a relationship with Him through Jesus Christ and empowered by His Spirit. It is not dependent upon any third-party theological treatise, no matter how good it may be.

The aim of E. W. Bullinger, admittedly a great scholar, was to simply point us back to the riches available to us in the Word of God itself and a relationship with the one true God therein revealed. We must keep this in mind when engaging in any study about the Scriptures. It is the study of the Scriptures in the proper context and in relationship to God, the Son, and the Holy Spirit that gives one life and power. A study about or even of the scriptures without this empowerment has the potential to be sterile.

As a final note on this subject, we find seven names for Jesus Christ in the book of Revelation concluding with Revelation 22:13. This one verse in many ways ties the whole of Scripture together.

"I Am the Alpha and the Omega, the First and the Last, the Beginning and the End." NLT

Group Warm-Up Questions

Which do you think is a more powerful motivator: love, fear or hate? Why?

How are all three of the above-mentioned motivators sometimes involved in a given situation? Please explain.

What popular figure alive today or from history used hate to motivate people?

When have you been motivated by love?

Read: 1 John 4:7-21

Reread: 1 John 4:7

What does John encourage his readers to do?

In fact, God uses John to tell believers to love each other fully three times in the primary verses we are studying today. We see this in:

1 John 4:7.

1 John 4:11.

1 John 4:12.

In the organization for effective communication known as Toastmasters International, members are instructed to make important points by telling their listeners what they want them to know three times. They are told to tell their audience what they are going to tell them, what they are telling them, and finally what they told them. The effectiveness of this technique is well-known. But where does this come from?

Like all truth we can find the roots of this in God's Word, which we of course call the Bible. His timeless truths are repeated time and again for our benefit in this wonderful Book.

That being said, what do you think God is trying to tell us by repeating this command three times in the space of a few lines of text?

Is this command also reiterated other places in the Word of God? Please explain and expound.

In point of fact, the word love is repeated hundreds of times in Scripture. Conversely, in the world, the word love is rarely used and even rarer still is its use in reference to the type of *agape* love we see spoken of in God's Word. A number of years ago, when reading a book presenting a comparative analysis of Islam, Judaism and Christianity, I was struck by the contrast we find in the patterns of thought found therein.

As already mentioned, love is found in abundance throughout the sacred text of Judaism and Christianity. However, in Islam this is different. There, we find that one is told to love Allah, but *never* instructed to love other adherents. In stark contrast, love is of paramount importance to fellow believers in Yeshua HaMaschiach, Jesus Christ, the Jewish Messiah.

How can we demonstrate our love for God?

Reread: 1 John 4:7-8

What is the relationship between loving God and knowing God?

Note 1: When used here the verb *know* is the same one used to describe the intimate union between husband and wife. It is much deeper than intellectual understanding. It is a matter of *perceiving* the truth. When one trusts Jesus Christ, they are born into His family. They receive His very nature. This is an ongoing daily experience of growth. Any argument to the contrary is proof positive that one does not really know God. We see this in:

2 Corinthians 5:17.

1 Peter 1:14-16.

2 Peter 1:4.

Note 2: In John's writings he characterizes the nature of God in three separate and yet interdependent ways. He writes:

1. God is spirit in John 4:24. He is beyond the restrictions of the physical world and not limited by time or space.

2. God is light in 1 John 1:5, which is a symbol of holiness. This is in contrast to the darkness of sin as discussed in John 3:18-21 and 1 John 1:5-10.

3. God is love in 1 John 4:8. While this concept is seen throughout Scripture, we should note that it is expressed in Lamentations 3:22-23 as never ceasing and in relationship to his faithfulness and mercy.

Reread: 1 John 4:9

Also read:

John 1:14

Romans 5:8

How did God show His love?

Why did God send His Son?

In 500 BC Socrates famously said, "It may be that the deity can forgive sins, but I do not see how."

Socrates, like Aristotle and many of their compatriots, was a very intelligent man. This is the line of great thinkers and intellectuals of which Paul the apostle was a member.

In any case, Socrates was on to something. He realized that there was no way sinful men and women could in any way pay for their sins in such a way as to propitiate such offenses. The only way for a sinful person to have their sins atoned for was for someone sinless to pay for them. In accordance with this line of reasoning, any sin that makes one unholy deserves death and can be atoned for only by the blood and death of a sinless personage. The death of a sinful person does nothing to atone for their sin as they deserve what they get.

What a predicament. Men and women by nature, even as recognized by Socrates and any honest thinker, cannot pay for their sins from the day they exit the womb forward as they are born into it.

One imagines that our adversary, Satan, was none too happy about God's plan to take care of this and make eternal life a possibility for us by the birth and atoning death of His Son. Like it or not, our adversary is intelligent and powerful. He was able to put two and three thousand together and understand what was prophesied in the Word of God. (I am using the numbers two and three thousand because that relates to the number of prophecies about the birth, death, resurrection and Second Coming of Jesus Christ in Judeo Christian Scriptures. All of them, _all of them_, regarding his birth, death and resurrection have already been fulfilled. Next up will be those that deal with His Second Coming. Please see _Composite Probability_ in the appendices of this book for more information on these exciting facts.)

How can we follow the example Jesus has set for us as stated in this verse?

Reread: 1 John 4:10

Also read: John 15:13-14

What is real love according to the Scriptures?

Do you have this kind of love for anyone? Please explain.

Would you be willing to lay down the life of your child for someone else?

Remember, this is essentially what God did for you and me.

Why or why not?

How does it make you feel that this was done most specifically for you?

What should be our response to this? (You may want to see John 15:14 as you contemplate your answer.)

Reread: 1 John 4:11

Why should believers love one another?

How should God's love motivate you to love others?

Reread: 1 John 4:12

What is the result of believers loving one another?

Reread: 1 John 4:13

How can believers know that they live in God and that God lives in them?

Reread: 1 John 4:14

To what did John testify?

Reread: 1 John 4:15

Also read: John 5:24

What happens when someone acknowledges that Jesus is the Son of God by making such a declaration and inviting Him into their heart and life?

How soon does this happen?

How would you explain what it means to live in God?

Reread: 1 John 4:16

How might you put this verse into your own words?

(If you are reviewing this in a small group study I suggest you have several members put this into equivalent words that are most meaningful to them.)

Reread: 1 John 4:17

What happens on an ongoing and continual basis to those who live in God as defined in the Word of God?

What is the result of this when we each face God on the Day of Judgment?

Note: It is of great value to realize the importance of the concept of excellence in the life of a believer. Please read and discuss the following verses.

Daniel 6:3

Joshua 1:8

Psalm 119:99

Proverbs 22:29

1 Timothy 6:11

James 1:4

2 Corinthians 13:5-13

Ephesians 6:7-8

Titus 2:7

Philippians 1:9-10

1 Peter 2:9

Philippians 1:6

2 Corinthians 7:1

2 Corinthians 8:7

2 Peter 1:3-4

2 Peter 1:5

Matthew 5:14-16

2 Timothy 3:16-17

Colossians 3:24-25

Philippians 4:8

Note 2: My wife Sally and I were privileged to know as friends and teach with both Harry and Marion Rich. Together they served as missionaries in some of the darkest places in Africa as well as in Haiti. Marion was the author of the books *Discovery: The Art of Leading Small Groups* and *Rejoice: You're a Minister's Wife*. Besides his missionary work and serving as one of the top officials in his denomination, Harry's primary literary work was an account of his adventures when he traveled to Rwanda in Africa during their civil war and genocide to provide aid to refugees. Having had the privilege of telling primitive peoples the good news of Jesus Christ they reported that when a person or family placed their trust in Jesus things began to change. They said:

Huts and houses were repaired.

Long neglected dwellings were cleaned.

Yards were either put in order or dedicated to raising food.

Farms were established to raise fish and other animals for food.

Husbands stopped beating wives.

Wives stopped cheating on husbands.

Husbands stopped cheating on wives.

People in general took better care of themselves and their children.

Children took care of elderly parents.

Elderly widows were looked after.

People no longer cheated each other at the market.

Honesty became the rule instead of the exception.

People treated each other with respect.

Is this not what we would expect from people who have begun to experience the new life in Christ as mentioned in John 10:10 and 2 Corinthians 5:17?

Since we know that the above verses are correct and that God's Word in the lives of people has results equivalent to what Harry and Marion Rich saw, what might we extrapolate when positive changes are not evident?

How does this relate to Matthew 7:17-23?

As a corollary to this I might add that in my study it appears that when in a culture people become new believers and study both the New and Old Testaments, they generally live the kind of increasingly excellent life we are discussing.

However, when they have only the New Testament, they tend to have less consistency than those who have the whole of God's Word.

Reread: 1 John 4:18

Are you afraid of anything?

If so, what?

If not, why not?

If we have fears, how can we overcome them?

What does perfect love do?

How and why does perfect love drive out all fear?

Reread: 1 John 4:19

Why should we love each other?

Note: This is written pointedly to believers.

Reread: 1 John 4:20-21

What is the relationship between loving God and loving other believers?

Why is it easier to love God than to love other believers?

When you have difficulty loving other believers, what is it that makes it hard?

How can we demonstrate our love for people who are not believers?

How can we demonstrate our love for other believers?

Application Questions

Who is someone you have a difficult time getting along with that you need to ask God to help you love this week?

What fear will you ask God to help you overcome?

What specific steps will you take this week to demonstrate your love for another believer?

Close in Prayer

WEEK 11

FAITH IN JESUS
1 JOHN 5:1-12

Open in Prayer

Group Warm-Up Questions

What makes a person's testimony seem credible or incredible?

How can one demonstrate love for their parents?

Is this sometimes hard to do?

Note: In the previous session we mentioned that there are at least four evidences that the love and life of a believer are being perfected. We covered the first two as found in:

1.   1 John 4:17-19 (Confidence).

2.   1 John 4:20-21 (Honesty).

In today's session we will discuss the next two evidences that God's love is present and being perfected. They are:

3.   Joyful Obedience (1 John 5:1-3).

4.   Victory (1 John 5:4-5).

Read: 1 John 5:1-12

Reread: 1 John 5:1

Who, according to God's Word, is a child of God?

What does the word "believe" mean in this context?

How do you then relate this to the term "believer"?

Note: Thesaurus.com defines a believer as:

1.   Someone who has confidence in the truth, existence, or reliability of something: *I am a firm believer that evolution happened the way that*

evolutionary biologists describe. The team's offensive coordinator is a big believer in the run game versus the passing game.

Note Aside: Please do not assume the first example of this concept indicates support for the spurious theory of evolution. I would refer you to Creation Truth Ministries in Canada for some excellent material on this controversial subject.

2. Someone who has or professes faith in something, especially a religion: *The church has grown from a handful of believers, meeting in the pastor's living room, to a congregation now in excess of 1,000.*

According to all of this, who is a believer in the context of what we call the Good News?

If this is so, why do so many people today insist on saying that everyone is a child of God?

How can you use this misstatement on the part of someone with whom you are speaking as a springboard to a positive conversation about Jesus Christ and trusting Him?

Reread: 1 John 5:1

What other observable trait does John say is evident in the life of a believer?

When have you seen this in action?

When have you met a believer who is new to you and felt an instant kinship? Please explain.

Why do you think this happens?

Reread: 1 John 5:2

What else do we learn is an observable trait of someone who is a believer?

What does it mean to obey God's commandments?

(**Note:** There are 613 commandments in the Old Testament alone.)

Please read the following verses as you construct your answer.

Exodus 20:2-17

Deuteronomy 5:6-21

Leviticus 21:8

Exodus 19:6

Leviticus 19:17-18

Mathew 22:37-39

Mark 12:30-31

Matthew 19:17-30

Galatians 5:22-23

1 Peter 1:13-2:3

In what way should we love the children of God?

Why is the reference from Galatians imperative if we are to obey God's commandments and adhere to His standard for us?

If someone claims to be a believer and does not overtly show it in their actions, what do we know about them?

How do you know that you are a child of God?

Reread: 1 John 5:3

1 Corinthians 10:13

How hard is it to keep God's commandments if we have appropriated the power of the Holy Spirit?

Can you think of a time when this impacted you? What happened?

Have you ever thought that God's commands were burdensome? How so?

What commands of God, if any, do you struggle with obeying?

As Dr. Charles Missler pointed out, the Bible is not merely a history book or text book. (Although it is supremely competent in fulfilling those roles.) It is also a love letter as we see in:

Psalm 119:14-16.

Psalm 119:54.

Psalm 119:97.

Psalm 119:103

Note: For a wonderful experience in the enjoyment and appreciation of God's Word I suggest you prayerfully read through Psalm 119.

Reread: 1 John 5:4

Who, and only who can defeat this evil world?

How is it that believers can do this?

What is the primary ingredient or ingredients that they need?

Reread: 1 John 5:5

Also read: 1 John 4:4

Who can win the battle against the world?

Why is it that only people in this category can defeat the world?

Note: Here we can see God's use of a great literary device. This shouldn't be too surprising since God did create the minds of humans and certainly knows how they work. The device mentioned for making a point that someone will remember is:

1. Tell them what you are going to tell them.

2. Tell them what you want to tell them.

3. Tell them what you told them.

Why do you think this is so effective in making an indelible impression on a person's mind?

Please think of another example of when you have seen this used.

What does it mean to you to overcome the world?

1.

2.

3.

4.

5.

6.

7.

In the investigation of this verse, we have been discussing overcoming the world. Of course, this implies and accepts that we are at war with forces that exist in opposition to God and in opposition to us.

Like it or not, we are in a war.

War is not easy and involves pain and suffering on the path to victory.

God's Word has some pointed things to say about fear, cowardice, bravery, and courage.

To understand this properly, let's take a look at the definition of the words, emotions, and actions we might consider in our discussion.

1. The Merriam Webster dictionary defines cowardice as "lack of courage or firmness of purpose."

2. It defines fear as "an unpleasant often strong emotion caused by anticipation or awareness of danger."

3. Conversely it defines courage as "mental or moral strength to <u>venture</u>, persevere, and withstand danger, fear, or difficulty."

4. It defines bravery as "the quality or state of having or showing mental or moral strength to face danger, fear, or difficulty."

Notice: Courage and bravery are not necessarily the absence of fear, but the proper facing of it.

Nelson Mandela reportedly said "I learned that courage was not the absence of fear, but the triumph over it. The brave man is not he who does not feel afraid, but he who conquers that fear." If this seems familiar, we should be aware that it is quite similar to what many courageous people have said over the centuries.

Please review the following biblical references and jot down what we learn about this in the Word of God:

Proverbs 28:1

Job 18:5-11

Matthew 10:28

Revelation 21:8

Matthew 10:33

1 John 4:18

Hebrews 13:5-6

Philippians 1:27

Deuteronomy 20:8

Deuteronomy 31:6

Proverbs 3:5-6

Proverbs 29:25

1 Corinthians 16:13

1 Corinthians 15:58

1 Chronicles 28:20

Ephesians 3:20

Philippians 4:13

Philippians 4:6

Romans 8:31

Joshua 1:9

Psalm 56:3-4

Isaiah 51:12

Isaiah 41:10-13

James 1:2-5

Psalm 31:24

Psalm 27:1

John 14:27

2 Timothy 1:7

Ephesians 6:10

Why do you think these concepts are so important in the Word of God and the life of a believer?

Reread: 1 John 5:6

How was Jesus revealed as God's Son?

Who confirms that Jesus is God's Son?

Reread: 1 John 5:7-8

What three witnesses agree that Jesus is God's Son and the Jewish Messiah?

Reread: 1 John 5:9

What is God's testimony about His Son?

Why is His testimony so much greater than human testimony?

Reread: 1 John 5:10

What do all who have trusted in the Son of God, Jesus, know about God's testimony?

What are those who choose to not believe God's testimony about His Son actually doing?

In what countless ways do we know that God's testimony about His Son is true?

Note: See *Composite Probability* in the appendices of this book as part of your answer.

1.

2.

3.

4.

5.

6.

7.

Why is it so preposterous for a human being to essentially call God a liar?

Reread: 1 John 5:11

What exactly has God testified about his Son?

Why is it so vitally important that we realize this?

Reread: 1 John 5:12

What all important truth do we find in this verse about life now and on an eternal basis?

Note: I strongly suggest that everyone, believer or not, understand and memorize this verse.

What is your relationship to the Son?

In your own words, how can a person receive eternal life?

Application Questions

How will you demonstrate your love for the Father (God) today?

What steps do you need to take in order to be certain you are a child of God?

What will you do to celebrate your life in the Son today?

Close in Prayer

WEEK 12

FINAL ENCOURAGEMENT
1 JOHN 5:13-21

Open in Prayer

Group Warm-Up Questions

What might make someone afraid to ask another person for something?

What sort of things do people today pin their hopes on?

Read: 1 John 5:13-21

Reread: 1 John 5:13

Why did John say he wrote this letter?

Please read:

1 John 5:18

1 John 5:20

John 10:10

John 14:6

1 John 2:23

1 John 5:12

John 5:24

How can we be confident that we have eternal life?

Note: There are generally two primary reasons people lack assurance of their place in the family of God, in what is called their salvation.

1. Some people do not have any empirical or actionable basis for such assurance. They have never entered into a personal relationship with Jesus Christ and regardless of any religious leanings or involvements **THEY DO NOT KNOW HIM.**

2. They do not know the Word of God, although they have invited Jesus into their life.

Hopeful Note: Both of these situations can be remedied. An unbeliever, church member or not, is invited into fellowship with Jesus Christ. (We see this concept in Revelation 3:20.) A believer who does not know the Word of God can, with the aid of the Holy Spirit, study and learn from this incalculably valuable resource. (We see this in 2 Timothy 3:16-17.)

Reread: 1 John 5:14-15

Also read:

Philippians 4:19

John 15:7

What confidence can believers have?

When might it be hard for someone to approach God with confidence? Why?

How can we know when something is according to God's will?

Note: A person can engage in great scholarly inquiry to be sure they are accessing God's will as discussed in Gordon Haresign's excellent book, *God's Will is Not Elusive.*

Even if someone does study Gordon's work or other excellent works of the sort, they still need to make use of the tools God has made available to us. Every believer should thirst for the knowledge that their lives and decisions reflect the will of God.

Good decision making for believers, while often complex, is characterized by several overriding characteristics and guided by the Holy Spirit. While each situation may seem unique to us, God provides us with the guidance we need in His Word. For some basics see:

1.   2 Timothy 3:16-17 for the primacy of God's Word.

2.   2 Timothy 1:7 regarding the involvement of the Holy Spirit

3.   Hebrews 10:25 for the importance of involving other competent, obedient and spirit filled believers as appropriate.

4.   1 Thessalonians 5:17 for the importance of prayer.

The following verses will add additional clarity to this.

Psalm 25:4-5

Psalm 25:8-9

Psalm 119:105

Proverbs 3:5-6

Proverbs 19:21

Jeremiah 29:10-14

Matthew 6:33

John 10:3-4

Romans 8:14

Romans 12:2

Ephesians 5:15-20

Philippians 2:12-13

1 Thessalonians 4:3-5

1 Timothy 2:3-4

Hebrews 10:35-36

Hebrews 13:20-21

And finally, one will do well to also study the principles in *How to Avoid Error* in the appendices of this book.

Reread: 1 John 5:16

Also read: Psalm 66:18

About what type of sin did John say his readers should pray?

About what type of sin did John say his readers should not pray?

Why do you think he said this?

Read: Jeremiah 7:16

All sin should be anathema to the believer. However, some sin is punishable by death and there is nothing we can do to prevent one from receiving their very just consequences.

As you think about this consider, and if you have time, discuss:

1. Nadab and Abihu in Leviticus 10:1-7.

2. Achan in Joshua 6-7.

3. Uzzah in 2 Samuel 6.

4. Ananias and Sapphira in Acts 5:1-11.

5. Improperly approaching communion in 1 Corinthians 11:30.

6. A business associate of mine claiming to be a devout Christian whose definition of sinful behavior when I confronted him about it was something for which he was caught. He ceased to be an associate of mine.

Reread: 1 John 5:17

What is the short definition of sin?

Why is it that some sin leads to death?

To what sort or sorts of death might sin lead?

What type of sin does not lead to death?

Reread: 1 John 5:18

What does a person who is a legitimate child of God stop doing?

Why does a person who is regenerated as someone who has trusted Jesus Christ change in this fashion?

Read the following verses as you construct your answer:

John 3:3

Romans 12:2

2 Corinthians 5:17

What sort of protection do those who have trusted Jesus Christ enjoy?

Reread: 1 John 5:19

Under whose control is the world around us?

Reread: 1 John 5:20

How is Jesus identified in this verse?

What has the Son of God done? Please make a list.

    1.

    2.

    3.

    4.

    5.

    6.

    7.

If we are children of God, under whose control are our lives?

Reread: 1 John 5:21

Also read: Proverbs 4:23

What last instruction did John give his readers?

Is this of importance today?

What sort of things in today's world might take God's place in someone's heart?

Why is this so important?

Read: Colossians 2:4

Against what did Paul admonish the believers in Colossae to guard?

What deceptive and clever arguments must believers guard themselves against in the world today? Please think of some examples.

What is the most effective way for believers today to be certain they do not fall prey to specious statements, practices, and philosophies?

Please read the following verses as you think about your answer and jot down what you see.

Psalm 119:105

Psalm 119:14

Psalm 119:114

Isaiah 55:11

Psalm 130:5

Proverbs 30:5

Psalm 119:11

John 16:12-14

Hebrews 10:24-25

2 Samuel 22:31

James 1:22

Luke 12:2

John 14:26

Genesis 2:18

Application Questions

What specific steps can you take today to place more confidence in God and less in the things of this world?

For what fellow believer who has sinned will you pray for today?

About what do you need to approach God more confidently?

What matter will you bring before God this week?

Close in Prayer

INTRODUCTION TO THE LETTER OF JUDE

In many ways I wish I had included the book of Jude with the Dynamic Studies book on Revelation.

However, the Dynamic Studies book on Revelation is long enough as is, so Jude fits in nicely at this point in time.

Jude is unique in that it was written about 2,000 years ago for today. It was written for what many call The End Times and for what seems to be the end of the Times of the Gentiles.

Of course, the book is not for the end of time, as time will continue on after the things dealt with have transpired. That being said, time as we know it is a human construct and it should inspire awe within us as we realize that God, who inspired the writing of the book of Jude through His Spirit, exists outside of the dimension and constraints of time.

The book deals with a time that is called the *Apostia*, the great falling away. During this time many will refuse to listen to sound doctrine and be attracted to false teachers and heresies referenced in 2 Peter 2:1 and 2 Peter 3:3.

It is, in fact, a sort of introductory hallway to the book of Revelation. As such, study of the book itself is an important part of a believer's education and preparatory arming for what is to come. The many Old Testament allusions that fill the book make it quite encompassing and fascinating.

Sadly, this gem of information as communicated to us by an infinite God is most often neglected today. Many people have not read the book and more still have not even heard of it or think it was about Judas. (Jude was actually one of four brothers of Jesus.) We do not wish to repeat those errors.

At this point I welcome you into a peek at the behind-the-scenes action in our world and the times to come.

Every believer should study this book to understand the tactics of our enemy and stand against them.

DOOM OF GODLESS MEN
JUDE 1-16

Open in Prayer

Group Warm-Up Questions

Who was someone everyone tried to avoid in grade school? Why?

What is something you have learned or taken note of from history?

Read: Jude 1-6

Reread: Jude 1

How did the author of this letter describe himself?

1.

2.

Reread: Jude 2

What did Jude first and foremost wish for his readers?

Why were and are these things so important as believers face a decaying world?

Reread: Jude 3

Why was Jude eagerly looking forward to writing this letter?

What happened to make Jude change directions and the subject of his letter?

When, where and how is it necessary for us to contend for the faith?

What responsibility do we have to protect the community of believers to which we belong against godless people?

How can we do so?

Can you think of an example when this was done properly and with success? What happened?

Can you think of an example when this was not done properly and without success, perhaps to avoid confrontation and conflict? What happened?

Reread: Jude 4

Why did Jude find it necessary to focus his letter differently than he initially intended?

Why did Jude describe certain people as godless or ungodly?

What things do you expect to see in a godless or ungodly person?

1.

2.

3.

4.

5.

6.

Read: Romans 6:1-2

How do ungodly or godless people misuse and abuse the grace of God?

Do such people sometimes worm their way into a fellowship of believers hoping to take advantage of people by misusing the hospitality and acceptance shown to them? How so?

Reread: Jude 5-7

Of what historical events did Jude remind his readers?

1.

2.

3.

4.

5.

6.

7.

How can it help us to remember things from the Bible, history or our own lives? Please explain.

What past events are most instructive and helpful to you to remember?

Reread: Jude 8

How do the things Jude brought to remembrance add to his warning about godless people?

What are some of the things godless people engage in that move them further from God?

1.

2.

3.

4.

Does their participation in these things move them further toward or even in to the camp of our enemy? How so?

Reread: Jude 9-10

What additional big mistake were these godless people making that such individuals still perpetuate today?

Why is this such a big and presumptuous mistake?

Reread: Jude 11

What ultimately destroys people who engage in such behavior without true repentance?

Read: 1 John 1:9

What can happen if they repent before it is too late?

At what point is it too late for such people?

(This is a very serious matter and the words we speak as well as the things we do carry great weight on an eternal basis.)

Read Hebrews 6:4-6 as you consider your answer.

Reread: Jude 12

Note: These godless people mentioned by Jude were actually in the fellowship and even taking communion. However, they were harming themselves and the real believers.

Jude reminds us of several ways these godless people are similar to things in nature. Please note each of these comparative analogies and then also note how they relate to the people under discussion.

1.   Comparative Illustration:

   • Impact:

2.   Comparative Illustration:

   • Impact:

3.   Comparative Illustration:

   • Impact:

4.   Comparative Illustration:

   •   Impact:

5.   Comparative Illustration:

   •   Impact:

6.   Comparative Illustration:

   •   Impact:

Read: 2 Peter 2:13-17

What else do we learn about the destructive and godless people who worked their way in among believers?

Reread: Jude 14-15

Enoch prophesied about these people and these times. Please enumerate the pronouncements God made through Enoch in these verses.

1.

2.

3.

4.

How does it make you feel to realize the seriousness of the offenses against God that He will ultimately call people to account for?

How can our knowledge of the certainty of future and eternal punishment motivate us now?

Why do you think God has provided this knowledge to us?

Psychologists tell us that the three of the greatest motivators are love, fear and greed. How do you see these coming into play in the spiritual and physical realms today for:

1.   Unbelievers?

2.   Believers?

Reread: Jude 16

What further characteristics of these people does Jude enumerate?

1.

2.

3.

4.

5.

We are not herein attempting to make a list of sins. We are, like God's Word, attempting to understand the characteristics evidenced by godless people.

Comparatively and conversely, we see what is called the Fruit of the Spirit enumerated in Galatians 5:22-23. How would you describe the contrast we see in your own words?

What happens when people engage in the ungodly thought patterns and modes of behavior described in today's primary passage?

How does this impact people around them?

How does this impact relationships?

How does this impact society at large?

How does this impact their city, state and country?

What happens when people are filled with the Holy Spirit and evidence its fruit in their lives?

How does this impact people around them?

How does this impact relationships?

How does this impact society at large?

How does this impact their city, state and country?

How can we be sure to prevent ourselves from being negatively self-absorbed as the people Jude warned us against were?

How can we prevent ourselves from grumbling, boasting, fault-finding, and flattering for our own advantage?

At this point, with the guidance of God's Word, we have established that:

1. Ungodly people will attempt with success to worm their way into groups of sincere believers.

2. Ungodly people who have infiltrated groups of sincere believers are destructive not only to themselves, but to the group they have infiltrated.

3. Believers are to act quite differently than the ungodly infiltrators as the Holy Spirit empowers the true believers.

But what then?

Believers must deal with the ungodly infiltrators when they are found in a fellowship just as a healthy government and country must deal with spies.

Consider the following:

Read: 1 Timothy 1:19

What two primary directives did Paul give Timothy?

1.

2.

Does this also apply to us today? How so?

This verse says that some people have deliberately violated their consciences. How might they have done this?

What is the significance of the Scripture telling us that this violation of their consciences was "deliberate?"

Why is it so important that we realize this violation was an overt action of the will of these people?

What was the result when these people violated their consciences?

What do you take this to mean?

What happens when people do this today? Please think of an example and discuss:

1. What it means for the people who do this.

2. What it means for the community of believers with whom they are associated.

3. How it impacts the non-believers who are always observing the lives of believers.

Read: Philippians 4:8

This verse taken in concert with 1 Timothy 1:19 infers that clinging to one's faith in Jesus and keeping one's conscience clear is also a matter of the will. What are your thoughts about this?

Read: 1 Timothy 1:20

What two examples does Paul give of people who violated their consciences?

What two actions did Paul take when these people made such a negative choice?

Note: In this type of instance, it appears that the type of people in question have made an overt decision to go beyond the remedies available to them as referenced in:

James 5:16

Romans 12:2

Read:

Proverbs 13:20

Proverbs 14:7

Proverbs 25:26

Psalm 1:1-4

Psalm 119:115

Psalm 26:4-5

1 Corinthians 5:11-13

1 Corinthians 15:13

2 Corinthians 6:14

2 Peter 3:17

Numbers 16:1-35

How should we respond today when people in a group of believers also make such negative choices?

If we respond in accordance with Scripture as Paul did, what impact does it have upon the faithful believers in the group?

How does it impact a group of believers if we respond in direct contradiction to the Scriptures in a disobedient and weak-minded fashion allowing these people to remain as active participants, treating them as legitimate and faithful followers?

How does it impact the effectiveness of the group if these people who have violated and continue to violate their consciences are seen by nonbelievers as representatives of what it means to be followers of Jesus?

Please discuss examples of when you have seen this handled in both ways and the impact it had.

Application Questions

How can you keep past events that teach you to live for God at the forefront of your thinking this week?

What steps can you take this week to guard against grumbling, faultfinding, boasting, or using flattery?

In what specific ways to you need to contend for your faith this week?

What could you do in the near future to find a greater appreciation for God's grace?

Close in Prayer

WEEK 14

ENDEAVOR TO PERSEVERE
JUDE 17-25

Open in Prayer

Group Warm-Up Questions

What is it like to anticipate an exciting, important event?

Who is the most difficult co-worker or boss you have ever had to deal with?

Read: Jude 17-25

Reread: Jude 17

What did Jude urge his readers to remember?

Why do you think he particularly wanted them to remember this?

Reread: Jude 18

What would Jude say would be the primary activities of ungodly people in the last days?

    1.

    2.

What did he say would be their motivation for this?

Do you see people in the world today seeming to act out of this same motivation and engage in the same type of activities? How so?

Note: Recently, the ten-year-old granddaughter of a couple we know went to visit her grandparents. She had just been in the care of her mother. They said the child told them that after talking with her mother, she thought she should have her uterus removed so that she would be unfettered in her enjoyment of life.

Do you think this is prima facie evidence of the trends Jude was speaking of in the world as things progress in the historical fashion predicted in the Scriptures? How so?

By the way, if you have the sort of background my wife and I have you are likely as astonished and aghast as we in hearing this come out of any human being.

Reread: Jude 18-19

In general, what are scoffers like?

Note: Vocabulary.com defines a scoffer as someone who jeers or mocks or treats something with contempt or calls out against the thing in question with which they vociferously disagree.

How do you relate this to the scoffers mentioned in Jude 18-19?

What were they scoffing at and how does it appear they were doing it?

Read:

Colossians 4:5-6

Colossians 3:23-24

How can believers turn the table on scoffers?

Can a believer make true statements or ask questions to make such people think and thereby:

1.   Point out the absurdity of the position of the scoffer?

2.   Point out the absurdity of neglecting or not accepting not only the forgiveness but the fullness of life available to believers?

In our short reading of the two above references in Colossians, we can see that the apostle Paul was doing just this.

Please think about this, how we might handle such situations, and the effective things we might say. Please jot down your thoughts here.

We should also realize that we are in a better position than the scoffers in this interchange.

Read Luke 12:11-12 and Matthew 10:19-20 to see what God promises us as we share our faith.

Note: This has been done in many effective ways over the centuries. I have been privy to have been:

1.   Observing the Father of Christian Rock, Larry Norman, in concert before a decidedly unbelieving and seemingly antagonistic audience. He changed the words to a song he was performing to:

   Stranger you can laugh;
   You can say that we're just fools.
   But I bet you won't be laughing,
   When He's handing out those jewels.

   Larry was speaking of the final judgment and went on to discuss it between songs to make a point.

2.   Sponsoring a debate between an antagonistic college professor who caused problems for many students with his relativistic and hedonistic encouragements against John Gerstner, a supremely intelligent and facile professor from a seminary. Try as he might to score some kind of point, the troublesome professor was unable to make a single point when confronted

with the truth of God's Word and someone skillful at presenting it with superior academic credentials behind him.

3. Seeing Paul Anderson, the strongest man in recorded history, perform and speak. I say it in this fashion as Paul often had to actually perform feats of strength right before the eyes of antagonistic and arrogant athletes before they would listen to him expound on God's Word.

4. In a debate in which I was involved in an honors English class about the efficacy of the Judeo-Christian Scriptures. I won when somehow, and I believe it was through the power of the Holy Spirit, God brought to my mind a simple and yet profound quote from Aristotle about the efficacy in practice of legitimate life principles. (They work so they must be valid.)

In each of the above scenarios we should note that the believing speaker first had to gain the respect of their audience by evincing competence at something the hearers held in high esteem.

Going back to the verses we cited from Colossians, how does God utilize this same technique with us even if our competence does not extend to the field in which those observing us operate?

Reread: Jude 20-21

Also read: Ephesians 6:10-18

What can and should believers do as they not only face daily life, but prepare for "combat" with an unbelieving world?

1.

2.

3.

4.

5.

6.

7.

8.

9.

10.

Reread: Jude 22

How should we as believers, having used the tools and spiritual weapons God has provided, respond to those who are having trouble with their faith because of the attacks of the enemy?

Who are some scoffers you must work or associate with?

How should you respond to the scoffers you associate or work with?

Reread: Jude 23

Also read: Philippians 2:14-16

How should we comport ourselves as we help believers having some difficulty come to a place of obedience to God's Word and the fullness of life (see John 10:10) He offers?

Speaking on a practical basis, how can we do this?

Read: 1 Corinthians 10:13

What great advantage do we have as believers as we engage in this conflict?

Can you think of times when this occurred in your life? What happened?

Reread: Jude 24

Who is able to keep us from falling as we bring the Words of Life to the world?

Reread: Jude 25

Why is He able to do this?

Please enumerate the characteristics that enable Him do this.

1.

2.

3.

4.

5.

6.

7.

How can we build up our faith?

Note: Our faith muscles or competences are like our bodies. We can become stronger and better by exercising our "faith muscles." Every good physical fitness program has a number of important components. These might include:

1. A good diet.

2. A regular workout regimen.

3. Periodic training with others.

4. Periodic game days.

5. Positive mental attitude.

The components of a healthy fitness regimen have parallels in our spiritual lives. We might think of this as:

1. A good diet (daily prayer and Bible reading).

2. A regular workout regimen (daily prayer and Bible reading and sharing the fruits with others by virtue of a life well-lived, in concert with God's Word).

3. Periodic training with others (fellowship).

4. Periodic game days (sharing our faith with others in a positive and victorious fashion in different situations).

5. Positive mental attitude (as a result of being filled with the Holy Spirit).

What, if anything, might you add to the above lists?

Reread: Jude 25

Why might this be a good verse for every believer to memorize and make a part of their daily prayer life?

Application Questions

What do you want to remember the next time you must deal with a difficult person who is not a believer?

How can you show mercy to a believer you know who may be doubting their faith?

What can you do to build up your faith this week?

Close in Prayer

APPENDIX 1

HOW TO AVOID ERROR

(Partially excerpted from *The Road to Holocaust* by Hal Lindsey)

1. The most important single principle in determining the true meaning of any doctrine of our faith is that we start with the clear statements of the Scriptures that specifically apply to it, and use those to interpret the parables, allegories and obscure passages. This allows Scripture to interpret Scripture. The Dominionists (and others seeking to bend Scripture to suit their purposes) frequently reverse this order, seeking to interpret the clear passages using obscure passages, parables and allegories.

2. The second most important principle is to consistently interpret by the literal, grammatical, historical method. This means the following:

   1. Each word should be interpreted in light of its normal, ordinary usage that was accepted in the times in which it was written.

   2. Each sentence should be interpreted according to the rules of grammar and syntax normally accepted when the document was written.

   3. Each passage should also be interpreted in light of its historical and cultural environment.

Most false doctrines and heresy of Church history can be traced to a failure to adhere to these principles. Church history is filled with examples of disasters and wrecked lives wrought by men failing to base their doctrine, faith, and practice upon these two principles.

The Reformation, more than anything else, was caused by an embracing of the literal, grammatical, and historical method of interpretation, and a discarding of the allegorical method. The allegorical system had veiled the Church's understanding of many vital truths for nearly a thousand years.

Note 1: It is important to note that this is how Jesus interpreted Scripture. He interpreted literally, grammatically, and recognized double reference in prophecy.

Note 2: It is likewise important that we view Scripture as a whole. Everything we read in God's Word is part of a cohesive, consistent, integrated message system. Every part of Scripture fits in perfectly with the whole of Scripture if we read, understand, and study it properly.

Note 3: Remember to **<u>Appropriate the power of The Holy Spirit</u>.**

Read: Luke 11:11-13

Read: Luke 24:49

Read: John 7:38-39

Read: John 14:14-17, 26

Read: I Timothy 4:15-16

Read: II Peter 2:1

Read: Mark 13:22

APPENDIX 2

UNDERSTANDING COMPOSITE PROBABILITY AND APPLYING IT TO THE JUDEO-CHRISTIAN SCRIPTURES

Before proceeding we might briefly reflect upon the reliability of the Judeo-Christian Scriptures. All honest researchers into their veracity have found that, as historical documents, they are without parallel. They are the most reliable and incontrovertibly accurate documents available in the world today. This has been the conclusion of all the erudite scholars and investigators who have taken the time to delve into this topic. For more information on this subject you may wish to read *The Case For Christ* by Lee Stroebel, *More Than a Carpenter* by Josh McDowell, and the *Evidence That Demands a Verdict* series, also by Josh McDowell. This is, of course, a very short list of the volumes available. A great deal of augmentative and corroborative material is available in such volume that if one were so inclined they might spend a lifetime in its study.

To better understand one of the ways the Creator of the Universe has validated His Word and the work and person of Jesus Christ, it is helpful to get a grasp on composite probability theory and its application to the Judeo-Christian Scriptures.

We are indebted to Peter W. Stoner, past chairman of the Department of Mathematics and Astronomy at Pasadena City College as well as to Dr. Robert

C. Newman with his Ph.D. in astrophysics from Cornell University for the initial statistical work on this topic. Their joint efforts on composite probability theory were first published in the book *Science Speaks.*

Composite Probability Theory

If something has a 1 in 10 chance of occurring, that is easy for us to understand. It means that 10 percent of the time, the event will happen. However, when we calculate the probability of several different events occurring at the same time, the odds of that happening increase exponentially. This is the basic premise behind composite probability theory.

If two events have a 1 in 10 chance of happening, the chance that both of these events will occur is 1 in 10 x 10, or 1 in 100. To show this numerically this probability would be 1 in 10^2, with the superscript indicating how many tens are being multiplied. If we have 10^3, it means that we have a number of 1000. Thus 10^4 is equivalent to 10,000 and so on. This is referred to as 10 to the first power, 10 to the second power, 10 to the third power, and so on.

For example, let's assume that there are ten people in a room. If one of the ten is left handed and one of the ten has red hair, the probability that any one person in the room will be left handed and have red hair is one in one hundred.

We can apply this model to the prophecy revealed in the Bible to figure out the mathematical chances of Jesus' birth, life and death, in addition to many other events occurring in the New Testament by chance. To demonstrate this, we will consider eight prophecies about Jesus and assign a probability of them occurring individually by chance. To eliminate any disagreement, we will be much more limiting than is necessary. Furthermore, we will use the prophecies that are arguably the most unlikely to be fulfilled by chance. I think you will agree that in doing so, we are severely handicapping ourselves.

1. The first prophecy from Micah 5:2 says, "But you, O Bethlehem Ephrathah, are only a small village in Judah. Yet a ruler of Israel will come from you, one whose origins are from the distant past" (NLT). This prophecy tells us that the Messiah will be born in Bethlehem. What is the chance of that actually occurring? As we consider this, we also have to ask: What is the probability that anyone in the history of the world might be born in this obscure town? When we take into account all of the people who ever lived, this might conservatively be 1 in 200,000.

Amazingly, about 700 years after this prophecy was uttered it was fulfilled when Yeshua Ha-Maschiach (The Jewish Messiah), who we call Jesus, was born in exactly the place predicted. We see this in Luke 2:11 where it states "The Savior— yes, the Messiah, the Lord—has been born today in Bethlehem, the city of David" (NLT)!

2. Let's move on to the second prophecy in Zechariah 9:9: "Rejoice greatly, O people of Zion! Shout in triumph, O people of Jerusalem! Look, your King is coming to you. He is righteous and victorious, yet He is humble, riding on a donkey---even on a donkey's colt" (NLT). For our purposes, we can assume the chance that the Messiah (the King) riding into Jerusalem on a donkey might be 1 in 100. But, really, how many kings in the history of the world have actually done this?

The fulfillment of this particular prophecy 500 years later was so unnerving that Matthew, Mark, Luke and John all included it in their historical accounts. Matthew recorded it as "Tell the people of Jerusalem, 'Look, your King is coming to you. He is humble, riding on a donkey— riding on a donkey's colt' " (Matthew 21:5 NLT).

This appears in John's writings as "The next day, the news that Jesus was on the way to Jerusalem swept through the city. A large crowd of Passover visitors took palm branches and went down the road to meet him. They shouted, "Praise God!

Blessings on the one who comes in the name of the LORD! Hail to the King of Israel!" Jesus found a young donkey and rode on it, fulfilling the prophecy that said: "Don't be afraid, people of Jerusalem. Look, your King is coming, riding on a donkey's colt" (John 12:12–15 NLT).

3. The third prophecy is from Zechariah 11:12: "I said to them, 'If you like, give me my wages, whatever I am worth; but only if you want to.' So they counted out for my wages thirty pieces of silver" (NLT). What is the chance that someone would be betrayed and the price of that betrayal would be thirty pieces of silver? For our purposes, let's assume the chance that anyone in the history of the world would be betrayed for thirty pieces of silver might be 1 in 1,000.

As unlikely as it may have seemed on the surface, this prediction was fulfilled approximately 500 years later and was noted by Matthew with the language itself being eerily similar to what had been written so many years ago. The NLT shows this as "How much will you pay me to betray Jesus to you? And they gave him thirty pieces of silver." (Matthew 26:15) How shocking would it be if you found that someone predicted exactly what you were going to spend for your next dinner out 500 years ago?

4. The fourth prophecy comes from Zechariah 11:13: "And the Lord said to me, 'Throw it to the potter'---this magnificent sum at which they valued me! So I took the thirty coins and threw them to the potter in the Temple of the Lord" (NLT). Now we need to consider what the chances would be that a temple and a potter would be involved in someone's betrayal. For our statistical model, let's assume this is 1 in 100,000.

This prophecy and its fulfillment is a continuation and completion of the one immediately prior to it in which the exact amount of the bribe for the betrayal of the Jewish King was predicted, again 500 years before it occurred. Here we find predicted not only the betrayal and the exact payment, but the actual usage of the funds. Matthew records fulfillment of this whole process as "I have sinned," he declared, "for I have betrayed an innocent man." "What do we care?" they retorted. "That's your problem." Then Judas threw the silver coins down in the Temple and went out and hanged himself. The leading priests picked up the coins. "It wouldn't be right to put this money in the Temple treasury," they said, "since it was payment for murder." After some discussion they finally decided to buy the potter's field, and they made it into a cemetery for foreigners (Matthew 27:4-7 NLT).

5.   The fifth prophecy in Zechariah 13:6 reads: "And one shall say unto him, What are these wounds in thine hands? Then he shall answer, Those with which I was wounded in the house of my friends" (KJV). The question here is, "How many people in the history of the world have died with wounds in their hands?" I believe we can safely assume the chance of any person dying with wounds in his or her hands is somewhat greater than 1 in 1,000.

Again, 500 years later we see this specific prophecy fulfilled and the evidence viewed by Jesus's disciples in John 20:20 where it says "As he spoke, he showed them the wounds in his hands and his side. They were filled with joy when they saw the Lord" (NLT)!

6.   The sixth prophecy in Isaiah 53:7 states, "He was oppressed and treated harshly, yet he never said a word. He was led like a lamb to the slaughter. And as a sheep is silent before the shearers, he did not open his mouth" (NLT). This raises a particularly tough question. How many people in the history of the world can we imagine being put on trial, knowing they were innocent, without making one statement in their defense? For our statistical model, let's say this is 1 in 1,000, although it is pretty hard to imagine.

In this case, approximately 700 years passed between the time the prediction was made and we see it fulfilled in Mark 15:3-5. There it is recorded as "Then the leading priests kept accusing him of many crimes, and Pilate asked him, "Aren't you going to answer them? What about all these charges they are bringing against you?" But Jesus said nothing, much to Pilate's surprise" (NLT).

7.   Moving on to the seventh prophecy, Isaiah 53:9 says "He had done no wrong and had never deceived anyone. But he was buried like a criminal; he was put in a rich man's grave" (NLT). Here we need to consider how many people, out of all the good individuals in the world who have died, have died a criminal's death and been buried in a rich person's grave. These people died out of place. (Some might also infer that they were buried out of place, though that is not necessarily true.) Let's assume the chance of a good person dying as a criminal and being buried with the rich is about 1 in 1,000.

Again we find that 700 years passed between the prediction of this event and the actual occurrence. Again, this event was so momentous that it was recorded by Matthew, Mark, Luke and John. Astonishingly, we find that he was placed in the tomb by not just one person of wealth, but by two. Joseph of Arimathea and Nicodemus, two of the wealthiest men in the region, worked together and laid the body in Joseph's own tomb. Matthew 27:60, speaking of Joseph of Arimathea's part in entombing Jesus' body says "He placed it in his own new tomb, which had been carved out of the rock. Then he rolled a great stone across the entrance and left" (NLT).

8.   The eighth and final prophecy is from Psalm 22:16: "My enemies surround me like a pack of dogs; an evil gang closes in on me. They have pierced my hands and feet" (NLT). Remember this passage and all the other prophetic references to the crucifixion were written before this form of execution was invented. However, for our purposes, we just need

to consider the probability of someone in the history of the world being executed by crucifixion. Certainly, Jesus wasn't the only person killed by being crucified. We will say that the chances of a person dying from this specific form of execution to be at 1 in 10,000.

Here we might note that Psalm 22 was penned by King David approximately 1000 years prior to the birth of Jesus. The word "crucifixion" and its derivatives had not yet been coined, but we see the process described in detail. Again, because of the import of this event it is recorded by each of the Gospel writers. In Mark 16:6 we see the fulfillment of the ancient prophecy and more where we read "Don't be alarmed. You are looking for Jesus of Nazareth, who was crucified. He isn't here! He is risen from the dead! Look, this is where they laid his body" (NLT).

Calculating the Results

To determine the chance that all these things would happen to the same person by chance, we simply need to multiply the fraction of each of the eight probabilities. When we do, we get a chance of 1 in 10^{28}. In other words, the probability is 1 in 10,000,000,000,000,000,000,000,000,000.

Would you bet against these odds?

Unfortunately, there is another blow coming for those who do not believe the Bible is true or Jesus is who He said He was. There are not just eight prophecies of this nature in the Bible that were fulfilled in Jesus Christ------there are *more than three hundred* such prophecies in the Old Testament. The prophecies we looked at were just the ones that we could *most easily* show fulfilled.

If we deal with only forty-eight prophecies about Jesus, based on the above numbers, the chance that Jesus is not who He said He was or the Bible is not true is 1 in 10^{168}. This is a larger number than most of us can grasp (though you may want to try to write it sometime). To give you some perspective on just how big this number is, consider these statistics from the book *Science Speaks* by Peter Stoner:

- If the state of Texas were buried in silver dollars two feet deep, it would be covered by 10^{17} silver dollars.

- In the history of the world, only 10^{11} people have supposedly ever lived. (I don't know who counted this.)

- There are 10^{17} seconds in 1 billion years.

- Scientists tell us that there are 10^{66} atoms in the universe and 10^{80} particles in the universe.

- Looking at just forty-eight prophecies out of more than three hundred, there is only a 1 in 10^{168} chance of Jesus not being who He said He was or of the Bible being wrong.

In probability theory, the threshold for an occurrence being absurd---translate that as "impossible"---is only 10^{50}. No thinking person who understands these probabilities can deny the reality of our faith or the Bible based on intellect. Every person who has set out to disprove the Judeo-Christian Scriptures on an empirical basis has ended up proving the Bible's authenticity and has, in most cases, become a believer.

These facts are more certain than any others in the world. However, not everyone who has come to realize the reliability and reality of these documents has become a believer. These intelligent people who understand the statistical impossibility that Jesus was not who He claimed to be and who yet do not make a decision for Christ are not senseless; they generally just have other issues. They allow these issues to stop them from enjoying the many experiential benefits that God offers them through His Word and the dynamic relationship they could have with Him, not to mention longer-term benefits. These people, of course, deserve love and prayer, because this is not just a matter of the intellect. If it were, every intelligent inquirer would be a believer. Rather, it is very much a matter of the heart, the emotions, and the spirit.

The truth of this statement was brought home to me in one very poignant situation. In this case, someone very near and dear to me said, "But Dad, this could have been anybody." No, this could not have been just anybody. The chance these prophecies could have been fulfilled in one person is so remote as to be absurd. That is impossible. Only one person in human history fulfilled these prophecies and that person is Jesus Christ. To claim otherwise is not intelligent, it is not smart, it is not well-considered, and it is not honest. It may be emotionally satisfying, but in all other respects it is self-delusional.

Printed in the United States
by Baker & Taylor Publisher Services